MW01273058

Feb 14

Dear Jenn

As your beautiful love story continues to unfold with Sir Christopher I thought you would enjoy this little book of love and be inspired. You two should probably be included in this book with all you do for your family but... 2nd edition!

Love you
Happy b-day
Gaby

WHAT THEY DID FOR LOVE

THE EXTRAORDINARY WAYS PEOPLE
EXPRESS THE HEART'S FINEST EMOTION

Reader's
digest

The Reader's Digest Association, Inc.

New York, NY / Montreal

A READER'S DIGEST BOOK

Copyright © 2014 The Reader's Digest Association, Inc.

The credits that appear on pages 215–216 are hereby made part of this copyright page.

Library of Congress Cataloging-in-Publication Data
What they did for love : the extraordinary ways ordinary people express the heart's finest emotion / editors of Reader's Digest.
    pages cm
  ISBN 978-1-62145-136-5 (hardback) -- ISBN 978-1-62145-147-1 (e pub)
 1. Love--Literary collections. I. Reader's Digest Association. II. Reader's digest.
 PN6071.L7W46 2014
 808.8'03543--dc23
                              2013032848

We are committed to both the quality of our products and the service we provide to our customers. We value your comments, so please feel free to contact us.

> The Reader's Digest Association, Inc.
> Adult Trade Publishing
> 44 South Broadway
> White Plains, NY 10601

For more Reader's Digest products and information, visit our website:
> www.rd.com (in the United States)
> www.readersdigest.ca (in Canada)

Printed in the United States of America

10 9 8 7 6 5 4 3 2 1

CONTENTS

ANIMALS WE LOVE

FOR THE LOVE OF STRANGERS

INTRODUCTION

Love comes in many forms and touches all of our lives— sometimes in grand, romantic ways, and other times in the smallest of gestures that forever touch our hearts. If we are lucky in life, we experience the love of family, friends, romantic partners, and possibly even the unconditional love of animals and the unexpected love of strangers.

Reader's Digest has been sharing love stories for decades, and we have sifted through the archives to find the most poignant love stories—tales that will bring you to tears and will renew your faith in the goodness of humanity. In these pages you'll meet a son who learns that the love between his father and him is more important than any political belief; you'll discover how the pure bond between a soldier and his dog mitigates the horrors of a war zone; and you'll see the generous spirit of a teenage organ donor whose tragic death provides the life-saving answer for dozens of people he never knew.

Love has the power to heal, transform, connect, and inspire. As you delve into *What They Did for Love*, we hope you'll be moved, touched, and inspired to follow your heart wherever it leads—around the world or maybe just around the corner.

A GREAT
ROMANCE

WHAT THEY DID FOR LOVE

BY ANDY SIMMONS

He Posted a Plea

On a Sunday evening last November, Patrick Moberg, 21, a website developer, was in the Union Square subway station in New York City. "Out of the corner of my eye, I noticed this girl," he says. "She had bright blue shorts and dark blue tights and a flower in the back of her hair."

New York's fun if you're a guy—the city's lousy with gorgeous women. But this one was different. She was his perfect girl. When the number 5 train pulled into the station, the two got on.

"I was enthralled," he says. "I noticed details like her braided hair and that she was writing in a pad. I couldn't shake the desire to talk to her."

Taking a deep breath, he headed her way. Just then the train pulled into the Bowling Green station. The doors opened, a rush of humanity swarmed in, and then suddenly, she was gone.

He considered giving chase, but there's a fine line between blind love and stalking. He thought of plastering the station with posters. Then a brainstorm: the Internet. "It seemed less encroaching," he says. "I didn't want to puncture her comfort zone."

That night, the world had a new website: nygirlofmydreams. com. On it, Patrick declared, "I Saw the Girl of My Dreams on the Subway Tonight." He drew a picture of the girl etched in his mind, along with a portrait of himself with this disclaimer pointed at his head: "Not insane."

The website spread virally, and soon he had thousands of leads. Some were cranks, and some were women offering themselves in case he struck out. Two days later, he got an e-mail from someone claiming to know the girl. He even supplied a photo. It was her. She was an Australian interning at a magazine, and her name was Camille. And she wanted to meet too.

Their first meeting was awkward. And why not? It was set up by *Good Morning America*. Like the rest of the media, GMA saw a great love story and pounced. But being sucked into a media maelstrom isn't necessarily conducive to a nascent love affair.

"There was a lot of uncertainty on how to act around each other," Patrick said. And in the back of Camille's mind, a nagging thought: Who is this guy?

The media circus eventually moved on, giving the two a chance to talk without a microphone present.

"Everything I found out about her was another wonderful thing," says Patrick. She was smart, funny and a big personality, a nice fit for this shy guy. "And," he continues quietly, "we've been hanging out together every day since." Thinking back, he sighs. "It's amazing everything went without a hitch."

He Got Her Jazzed

"I really can't think of anybody who wouldn't appreciate being met at the airport by a jazz band," says writer Calvin Trillin. "I suppose there might be some people who are in the witness protection program."

But Calvin's wife, Alice, wasn't some hood in hiding, and she would, he knew, most definitely love being feted by a jazz band.

The year was 1972, and Calvin was in Louisiana covering a crawfish festival. Back in New York, Alice's parents were both ill, and she was coming down for some much-needed R&R. Calvin wanted to cheer her up. He called a friend at Preservation Hall about getting a band. But Jazz Fest was in full swing. All the good ones were booked. So he took what was left.

When Alice's flight landed, she deplaned and walked smack into a wall of sound—brass, to be exact—tooting a rousing rendition of "Hello, Dolly!" For her. And she laughed.

"She saw it as a grand gesture. And I don't think she cared that the cornet player was actually an antiques dealer." In fact, he wasn't even from Cajun country. He hailed from London. And the trombone player? Norwegian. They happened to be in town for the festival.

Calvin and Alice strolled arm in arm through the terminal, trailed by their personal band blasting out standards. Along the way, passengers fell in behind and began second-lining all the way to the baggage area.

"Usually not the most interesting of times, waiting for your bags," says Calvin. "But they kept playing."

Alice died a few years ago, but Calvin clings to the memory of that day. "She was a very engaged person," he says. "Having a jazz band meet her fit her personality."

So what if he couldn't land a Satchmo or a Wynton Marsalis? As Calvin reminds us, "Imperfect gestures are still nice gestures."

He Puzzled Her

Aric Egmont knew he had to calm down or he was going to blow it. After all, who breaks out into a flop sweat doing the crossword puzzle? If he didn't relax, he was sure to clue his girlfriend, Jennie Bass, into the fact that this was no ordinary Sunday *Boston Globe*. This was his marriage proposal.

The two, both 29—he's in communications, she studies public health—had dated for four years and never seriously discussed marriage. Why mess up a good thing? went the thinking. But Aric had second thoughts. And since they were fanatics, he says, proposing via the tiny boxes of a crossword puzzle "was a more natural idea than it might seem to others."

So last June he contacted the Globe and told them about

his idea. They bit. Aric fed Globe puzzle writers Emily Cox and Henry Rathvon personal info to be turned into clues, then he waited . . . for four torturous months.

On the morning of September 23, having not slept the entire night before, Aric nonchalantly asked Jennie, "Want to do the crossword puzzle?" He bolted downstairs and out the door, grabbed the paper, then ran up to their bedroom. Climbing back into bed, the two assumed their normal puzzle-solving pose, with Jennie leaning against him. Almost immediately, she was struck by the number of clues that matched up with people and places in her life.

Twenty across asked: "Lover of Theseus." The answer was Ariadne, whose namesake is a friend of Jennie's. Seventy-three across: "One of the Judds." Naomi, also Jennie's sister's name. Ninety-one across: "NASCAR driver Almirola." Answer: Aric.

Aric began scanning ahead to where the big clue was. "I knew the moment was coming," he said. And there it was. One hundred eleven across: "Generic proposal." Clever, he thought, a wordplay on Jen and Aric. The clue next to it was "Winston's mother."

"Look at that," said Aric. "'Will you marry me, Jennie.'" He waited for a reaction. He didn't get one. Jennie is a smart person, smart enough to know all about Theseus' love life, but this was information overload. So Aric produced a ring and, quoting the *Boston Globe* crossword puzzle, asked, "Will you marry me, Jennie?"

After tears and shrieks and lots of "I love you's," Jennie said yes.

"I'm not the most romantic person," admits Aric. "I think I was playing above my head on this one."

Then Romeo adds, "Hopefully, this will satisfy Jennie for a while."

She Forgave

As blind dates go, it was a good one. The year was 1950, and some friends figured that 20-year-old Grace Miltenberger might like their fellow Marine, Bob. They were right. "I thought he was the most handsome man in the world, and I fell right in love with him," she says. It was mutual.

They dated happily for almost a year, then Bob up and disappeared. No calls, no visits and, most maddeningly, no explanations.

Not one to wallow, Grace enlisted in the Marines. Four years later, she and Bob hooked up again. Neither remembers the exact circumstances, but Grace does recall, "I still loved him." And after a few months, her finger sported a big, fat diamond engagement ring.

Then it happened again. In October 1954, she got a call from Bob saying he couldn't go through with it. No reason given; he just couldn't do it.

"The not knowing why is what hurt the most," says Grace.

As before, she collected herself. In 1958 she married another man, and over the years, the couple had five daughters. But the marriage was an unhappy one, and adding to Grace's anxiety was a secret she kept from her husband. Taped to the underside of a dresser drawer was the engagement ring Bob had given her. After what he put her through, most people might have pawned it or tossed it in a river. But not Grace. "I never stopped loving him," she says.

When her faltering marriage dissolved in 1969, Grace devoted herself to her daughters and to getting degrees in sociology and nursing.

Fast-forward to 2004. The phone rings. A voice says, "Gracie?"

"I threw the phone in the air and said, 'Oh, my God. It's Bob.'"

He'd called under the pretense of finding out where the guy who'd introduced them was buried. Three and a half hours later, they hung up. During their chat, Grace learned that Bob was a widower after 48 years of marriage.

"I never figured out what happened to us," he said at one point.

"I'll tell you what happened—you dumped me." But she wasn't mad. She was thrilled to be talking to him.

On New Year's Day 2005, they became engaged over the phone. Six months later, Bob visited Grace at her home outside Tulsa. It was the first time they'd seen each other in half a century. He showed up at her doorstep, and, she says, "we just walked into each other's arms like we'd always been together."

On the day he popped the question, Bob said, "Now I guess I've got to get you a ring."

"No," she said. "I've got one."

"Who gave you that?"

"You did, you big, dumb jerk. Fifty years ago."

This time, Bob didn't run away.

ALL THE DAYS
OF YOUR LIFE

BY NEIL SIMON
From *Rewrites: A Memoir*

My wife Joan and I were on vacation at a ranch near San Antonio, Texas. For three days we played tennis from morning till sundown, and we even got in a few rounds of golf. Nights were spent around a campfire, trading stories with friends.

On the fourth day Joan started to limp, holding her hip in pain. But this didn't stop her, and we played our hearts out until our last day there.

As a friend drove us to the airport for our trip back to New York, he said, "I don't like the look of that limp, Joanie," and cautioned her to see a doctor. Two days later our internist, Dr. Jack Bornstein, made an appointment for Joan to see a radiologist. She was in the X-ray room for about a half hour. Then we sat in the doctor's office, waiting.

When the doctor returned, he smiled at Joan and said he was still waiting for the plates to dry. Almost as an afterthought, he said, "Mr. Simon, I have some things to go over with you. Could you come inside?"

I shrugged to Joan and followed him into a back room with X rays on the wall. He pointed to a small gray area the size of a nickel. "This is her left hipbone. This dark gray area worries me."

I could feel my heartbeat quickening. "What do you mean, worries you? What do you think it is?"

"It looks like a small tumor. It's possibly benign, but we won't know until we do a biopsy."

When the doctor and I returned, Joan was sitting there. The doctor explained to her in carefully chosen words what he had told me. He would set up an appointment at Lenox Hill Hospital for a biopsy. It was a simple procedure in which they'd take a bone sample from her hip. After the tests they'd know better how to treat it.

This was in 1971 when cancer was a word still spoken in hushed voices. But the words "treat this" and "simple procedure" gave us cause to think that there really wasn't any concern.

I was nervous, but I couldn't believe anything was seriously wrong with Joan. We had been married nineteen years, and she looked robustly healthy and as beautiful as I had ever known her.

That night at dinner we said nothing to worry Ellen and Nancy, our two girls. Joan told them she might be out the next day when they came home from school because she had to take some tests for "this pesky leg of mine." That was all.

Later Joan got into bed next to me. "Are you worried?" she asked.

"Worried? No. Not at all."

"Would you tell me if you were?"

"Probably not. But I am not worried."

She turned on her side and closed her eyes. "Would you rub my back? It still hurts."

I rubbed her back as gently as I could.

The next day I was in the Lenox Hill waiting room with Joan's mother, Helen, when the surgeon appeared. "Mr. Simon?" he said.

I followed him down the hall to the privacy of a cold, back stairway. Sitting on the third step, he asked me to sit next to him.

"It's not good," he began.

"What do you mean? The biopsy?"

"In examining her before the procedure, I found a malignant tumor in her breast. It's cancer, and it's already metastasized. I didn't remove her breast."

The words were coming too fast, with too many emotions bouncing around in my brain to accept what he was saying. What was the prognosis? I heard it all in one devastating statement: "She has about a year. A year and a half at most."

A hole opened up underneath me. The fall was far and dark and unending. I could not breathe, and I could not stop sobbing. He put his hand on my arm and said he was sorry.

"Does she know?" I finally asked.

"I told her it was breast cancer. I did not tell her how long she has. That's as much a family matter as it is a medical one."

"What do I tell her?"

"I would give her some hope. She'll know herself when the

time comes. If I were you, I'd say that we caught the cancer early and that we got it all. If you can handle it, keep it from the children for a while. That's up to you, of course." He said he would do what he could to slow things down.

Joan was wheeled into her room, and the doctor went in. I saw Helen in the hallway. It wasn't fair to keep the truth from her. Besides, I knew that I couldn't get through it on my own, that I'd need an ally.

Helen's eyes looked into mine. I burst into tears and held onto her. She sobbed, saying over and over, "I knew it. I knew it all along."

I told her everything and explained how the doctor thought we should handle this. "It's just between us," I said. "I don't want anyone else to know. Not Ellen. Not Nancy. Not until it's time."

She nodded as the doctor summoned us into Joan's room. My wife was sitting up in bed, a hopeful smile on her face. "The doctor said they caught it early," she said. "They got it all. Isn't that wonderful?"

I nodded and kissed her. I could feel her body relax in my arms. From that moment I lived out a conspiracy of silence. Yet I still believed, no matter what I had been told, that Joan would beat the odds.

Joan started radiation treatments. As the weeks passed and her pain lessened, her spirits rose. I got so much in the habit of keeping up my own spirits that I didn't know if I was pretending or believing. The lie became the truth. Not the real truth, but one that gets you through day to day.

At home I worked on my new play, *The Sunshine Boys*, letting it swallow up all my other thoughts. The hours I sat over the typewriter were my refuge. Joan stayed in bed, writing poetry—something she had not done since college, almost twenty years before. I wanted to get something for Joan that would deflect the shadow that hung over her. I thought of the dream house she'd always wanted.

We had friends in Bedford, New York, about an hour's drive from the city. I rented a car and drove up, telling Joan I had meetings that day about some film projects.

I walked into a real-estate office, and within an hour I'd seen a dozen houses. About 3 p.m. we turned into a wooded area with a lovely little home sitting on a knoll. I saw a wooden footbridge over a stream. Beyond it the sun shimmered on a lake. "It's Blue Heron Lake," said the agent. "I'll show you."

He took me across the bridge to a small pier with a boathouse. A rowboat was tied to the rail. The lake seemed enormous.

I barely looked at the house before I made an offer, then went to his office and signed some papers. If Joan were happy here, who knew what miracles could occur?

Driving home, I wondered what Joan would think of my buying a house without her ever seeing it. It was so unlike me to do something like this. I walked into the bedroom, unable to conceal the huge smile on my face. She smiled back. "What are you so happy about?"

"I did something crazy today. Maybe something wonderful."

"Are you going to tell me?"

"I bought a house. On a lake. Do you think I'm crazy?"

The smile on her face was worth everything. "I don't believe it! Are you telling me the truth?"

We talked all night about the house. Nancy and Ellen were beside themselves with joy. When I turned out the lights, I wondered, Does she know why I did it so quickly? But even if she did suspect, her mind was now consumed with living in the country on a place so perfectly named as Blue Heron Lake.

I began to have the reverse of nightmares. My dreams were happy—of a healthy Joan, of meeting her for the first time at summer camp in the Pocono Mountains, of the laughter we shared sitting in Washington Square Park with our older daughter, Ellen, still in a baby carriage. I awoke feeling wonderful until I turned and saw Joan sleeping beside me, and the awakening became the nightmare.

She rarely let on to her own feelings. She never asked questions, and I soon learned to stop asking "How are you feeling?" She still couldn't get around without a cane, and I could see she didn't want me to help her. Still, when she was walking down the stairs, my hand was always an inch away from her arm.

At the next appointment with the oncologist, I was not prepared for what he said.

"Well, Mrs. Simon, everything looks good. The tumor is going into remission."

An enormous smile of relief crossed Joan's face. I could barely believe my ears. What was happening here? Was the cancer gone?

I no longer knew what to believe except that today the sun was shining and that Joan and I were going to leave for her first visit to the house in Bedford. When we arrived, she was beaming with excitement. "I'll show you the house in a minute," I said. "First comes the lake."

Joan stood on the dock, looking at the boathouse and the water. I could see by her expression that it took her back to when she was her happiest: growing up in the Poconos, taking a rowboat out at night and swimming in the dark, cool waters.

"I'm going to get rid of this cane," she said. "I'm going to swim in the lake. And I'm going to catch the biggest fish and cook it for dinner."

And that's exactly what she did.

By summer Joan was out in a boat fishing with Ellen and Nancy, teaching them what she learned as a girl. In the afternoons we played tennis. She was banging them across the net with power and speed. "Damn it!" she'd yell. "Hit the ball like you want to win!"

It was wonderful to see her like this again. The cane was gone. The limp was gone. We had our lives back. Had God granted us a reprieve?

At the end of the summer, Joan was still free of all signs of cancer. We went to Manhattan, and I started rehearsals on *The Sunshine Boys*. I was glad now I had never told Ellen and Nancy about Joan's recent battles, and I prayed I would never have to.

After the play opened, Joan and I took the girls to Florida. Suddenly the limp was back again. Joan held on to the railing when climbing steps, breathed a little harder, moved a little more slowly. A few days later the pain got sharper, and she could no longer get around without the cane.

Radiation treatments started again in Manhattan. At dinner Joan would use the word "treatments" but never mentioned radiology. She just tossed it off as that "bad leg" of hers. The girls seemed to accept it.

Finally one weekend in the middle of the night, Joan turned to me and whispered, "I'm so scared." I tried to assuage her fears, but we both knew the only true comfort I could give her was to hold her tightly until she fell asleep.

Joan's health was not improving, but radiation relieved the pain. In the spring the warm sun and fresh air put color back in her cheeks. Her smile returned, yet it was not the smile I had known all these years. It reflected a new attitude—not exactly acceptance but rather understanding, as if she had made a pact with someone that was going to get her through this.

I saw her walking in the woods with Nancy, who was ten, telling her how the flowers kept replenishing themselves and that even when a flower dies, it inevitably comes back in a new place. She was telling Nancy in her own way what I couldn't bring myself to say.

I was outside the house when I heard her cry of pain. I rushed into the bedroom and found her unable to move. I helped her into bed, then called Jack Bornstein, who said to get her into Lenox Hill.

I phoned for an ambulance, and Joan asked me to call her mother. The doctors in the hospital told me Joan would need to stay about a week.

Two weeks came and went. A month went by. When I met Dr. Bornstein in the hall, I saw the glum look on his face. "What's happening?" I asked.

"The cancer is spreading through her like wildfire," he said. "Faster than we can treat it. We'll do everything we can to make her comfortable. Let's not give up hope."

Joan did not want any visitors except for family. Even I couldn't go into her room without first knocking. The nurse would open the door a crack and whisper, "Joanie wants a few minutes to get ready."

"Even for me?"

"Especially for you."

When the door opened, Joan was sitting in bed, smiling her best smile, hair tied back in the ponytail she had worn when I first met her. She would talk about the girls, my work, even make plans for when she got out of the hospital.

One night at home I sat with Ellen at the kitchen table. Her 15-year-old face looked at me apprehensively. "I should have told you this before," I said. "You know Mom is really sick."

She nodded.

"I don't know how long she'll last. The doctors say it could be as long as August or even—"

"I knew she was sick. I knew she was going to die. I just didn't know when." Her eyes welled up with tears, and as I reached across the table to touch her hand, all her sorrow came pouring out. I told her I wouldn't say anything yet to Nancy, who was at camp. She was only two hours away, and I could bring her back before anything happened.

The phone rang on the table next to my bed. It was 3:10 a.m., July 11. A voice told me softly that Joan had passed away in her sleep.

She was 40 years old.

I sat up in bed, trying to compose myself, then woke Ellen. It came sooner than we expected, and the finality of it hadn't sunk in yet. The depth of the loss comes later, when the sun rises and you realize that this new day and all the days of your life to come will be without Joan.

I made the arrangements to bring Nancy home from camp. This was the day I finally told her, and it was too late. Of all the regrets I've ever had, what I most regret was not telling her sooner. It took her years to tell me she was angry and confused. Yet she never blamed me.

We drove home from the cemetery with Joan's mother sitting between her grandchildren. I looked at their faces and at the countryside passing by. At age 46, with two young daughters, I felt empty and frightened. The one thing we did have was each other.

TO MEND HER HUSBAND'S HEART

BY JOHN PEKKANEN

Floyd stokes stirred awake in the pitch-darkness, and immediately felt the autumn chill. The 57-year-old peanut farmer had never minded early mornings, and in fact for most of his life, he had relished spending eighteen-hour days in the fields. Now, though, he had to struggle just to get out of bed. Constricted arteries caused him chest pain that at times was almost unbearable.

"Floyd," his wife, Jean, whispered. "Why don't you rest a little longer?"

"No, I'm gettin' up. If I'm gonna die, I'd rather be on my feet than in bed."

Doctors had tried everything to mend Floyd's heart: triple coronary-bypass surgery, an arsenal of medications, a restrictive low-fat diet. Nothing had helped. Floyd's condition left him constantly exhausted and short of breath.

"This is no way to live," he'd told Jean.

As she listened to her husband's rapid, shallow gasps that October morning in 1997, Jean felt helpless and frightened. She and Floyd had been married for thirty-eight years. More than anything else, she wanted the two of them to grow old together. Now, as she watched Floyd walk slowly from the bedroom, Jean could sense that dream slipping away. She didn't know what she could do to save Floyd—she was a high school teacher in tiny De Leon, Texas, not a doctor. But she had to find help for the man she loved, and she had to find it soon.

Jean Wright was just a sixth-grader at De Leon Elementary when she developed a crush on Floyd Stokes. It took Floyd two years to notice the soft-eyed girl with wavy brown hair and ask her for a date, but when he did, they turned out to be a great fit. After going steady for two years, they married in June 1959.

Floyd was 19, Jean 17. To provide for his bride and the family they hoped would follow, Floyd first roughnecked in the Texas oil fields, then pumped gas at a filling station in De Leon. With their savings, the couple bought a 214-acre farm. Working seven days a week, often from sunrise until midnight, Floyd added more land and soon had five thousand acres under cultivation.

"Work feels natural to me," he told Jean. "It's what I love to do." In 1969, after their two sons—Floyd and David—entered school, Jean enrolled at a local state college, earning both a bachelor's degree and then a master's. She began teaching English at De Leon High School.

Their lives were full and rewarding until a cold day in December 1988. While repairing his farm combine, Floyd felt a crushing pain in his chest. At age 48, he had suffered a major heart attack. After they opened his chest for a triple bypass, the doctors discovered that Floyd had narrow coronary arteries, which were now diseased as well.

The surgery offered only temporary relief. After less than a decade had passed, two of Floyd's bypasses had virtually closed, and the third provided the front of his heart with only a minimal amount of blood. Despite medication, his pain and shortness of breath grew worse.

More surgery was out of the question, and Floyd's doctors held out little other hope. Watching her husband grow more and more ill might have paralyzed another woman, but it drove Jean into action: She would find a solution herself. Although she knew little about medicine, she began buying armloads of magazines and papers, combing them for news of cutting-edge coronary treatments.

And in late November 1997, she found it. In a newsmagazine, Jean read about a new form of gene therapy—angiogenesis— in which new blood vessels were grown in limbs that had lost their blood supply. The researcher, Dr. Jeffrey Isner of Boston, hoped to apply this therapy to human hearts.

"Floyd," she called out. "This may be what we've been praying for!"

Early the next morning, Jean phoned Dr. Isner's office. FDA approval of the therapy was still pending, an assistant told Jean, and even if they got the green light, no more than twenty patients would be accepted in the trial. Jean then phoned Floyd's cardiologist, who said he found Isner's research promising. But he added a warning: "The chances of Floyd getting into one of those clinical trials are about the same as winning the lottery."

Like Jean Stokes, Dr. Jeffrey Isner was also in search of answers. As a professor of medicine at Tufts University School of Medicine and chief of cardiovascular research at St. Elizabeth's Medical Center of Boston, Isner was driven to find a successful treatment for certain types of advanced, and so far incurable, vascular disease.

One new direction for research had presented itself in the early 1980s, when Dr. Judah Folkman's team at Children's Hospital Boston identified special proteins that formed the building blocks for blood vessels. Tumors employed these proteins, Folkman's research showed, to recruit a blood supply for themselves; this flow of blood, in turn, nourished the tumors. Folkman theorized that if he could somehow block these proteins and shut down the new blood vessels, the tumors would shrink and perhaps even die.

Isner now wanted to try a new application for Folkman's breakthrough. Wasn't it possible that these vessel-building proteins could also stimulate new vessel growth where it was needed? With grants from the National Institutes of Health, Isner focused on the VEGF (vascular-endothelial growth factor) gene. This gene produces cells that form the lining of blood vessels, the basic biological framework needed for new vessel growth.

Throughout the 1990s, Isner made huge strides in his research. In his first animal experiments, he tied off the leg arteries of rabbits to stop blood flow to their lower legs. He then injected the rabbits with VEGF genes, hoping this "saturation bombing" would get enough of the genes inside cells to do their job.

After a few weeks came what Isner called "one of those Eureka! moments." The rabbits had indeed developed a network of small vessels that carried blood to the tied-off area of their legs.

Isner was now eager to test the gene therapy on humans. In 1996 he received FDA approval for human experiments with VEGF genes on people suffering from advanced peripheral vascular disease. The results were stunning. For most of the twenty patients, the treatment not only saved their legs from amputation, but allowed them to walk again without pain.

One giant step remained: experimental gene therapy on the human heart. If FDA approval was granted, and if the therapy worked, the result could be "biological bypasses" for patients who had exhausted all other options—patients exactly like Floyd.

So many questions remained, though, and all of them preyed on Jean Stokes as she watched her husband grow weaker. For starters, Isner still did not have FDA approval for the experiment. Even if the FDA did approve, there was no guarantee that Floyd would be included in the trial. One night, overwhelmed with anxiety, Jean slipped out of bed. If Isner and his staff only knew Floyd, she thought, they couldn't possibly turn him down. So she began a letter to Isner, writing of her long and loving marriage to Floyd.

Later, she mailed another letter, telling how she and Floyd had looked everywhere for medical assistance but had found none. "We are desperate!" she wrote.

Their sense of urgency only heightened when they learned that Isner had received approval for testing his therapy—but, as he had cautioned, only for twenty heart patients. The next afternoon, Jean sent another letter to Isner's office. This time she included a picture of her husband, along with Floyd's medical records and a letter from his cardiologist. Two weeks later, Jean and Floyd were on a plane to Boston.

"So you're the peanut farmer from Texas," said Lorna Henshaw, Isner's patient liaison, when she was introduced to Floyd.

"How'd you know?" he asked.

Henshaw smiled. "I recognize you from your wife's picture."

Floyd looked at Jean. She had not told him about the picture or the clutch of letters she had sent.

Five days of tests and interviews ended with the conclusion that Floyd was indeed an excellent candidate for VEGF therapy. But that was hardly the end of it. For one thing, Isner wouldn't begin the experimental therapy for several weeks. So it was back to Texas, and the farm, and the waiting, and the pain.

Jean was haunted by the thought that Floyd might die at any moment, even as they drew so close to a possible treatment. Six weeks later Lorna Henshaw was on the phone. "Congratulations!" she said brightly. "You're in the program!"

Floyd and Jean flew to Boston on May 24, 1998. On the morning of Floyd's treatment, Jean left her hotel room at 2 a.m. and walked two blocks to his room at St. Elizabeth's.

"You mean everything to me," she told her husband in the darkness. "You've been my whole life."

"You've been the same to me," Floyd murmured. "You're the only reason I'm still here."

At 5 a.m. orderlies wheeled Floyd into the operating room. Worried that he might not survive general anesthesia, doctors administered a pain-killing spinal block instead.

With Isner alongside him, surgeon James Symes made a four-inch incision on Floyd's left side, between his two lower ribs. Meanwhile, holding a syringe filled with the VEGF genes in a clear liquid, he studied a fluoroscopic X ray of Floyd's chest and heart on an overhead monitor.

Keeping his eyes glued to the monitor, Symes maneuvered the long needle toward the left ventricle, one of the heart's two major pumping chambers. "Here we go," he announced, pushing the needle directly into Floyd's heart muscle, releasing billions of VEGF genes.

All eyes turned to the monitor. Floyd's heart continued to beat, and his vital signs remained stable. So far, so good, Isner thought. Next, Symes injected a second area of the left ventricle, then a third and fourth. Jean had spent the two-hour procedure sitting nervously in the waiting area.

Isner smiled as he walked in. "It went very well," he told her. Relieved, Jean also knew that she and Floyd had another excruciating wait ahead to see if the genes would work.

At first, nothing happened. In particular, the agonizing pains in Floyd's chest persisted. Isner had told Jean that the change—if it came at all—would take several weeks.

On a Sunday morning three weeks later, Floyd awoke with a start. There was a sensation in his chest that he hadn't felt in years. He edged out of bed and took a deep breath. What a strange, wonderful feeling: his lungs were filling with air. He moved around and bent over—still, there was no pain.

"Jean!" Floyd called out. "I can breathe deeply again!"

A few days later Jean watched in happy amazement as Floyd headed outside. "Got a few things that need doing," he said. Hopping into his pickup, he drove off to check his peanut crop. Jean smiled. The man she loved—the man who was her life— was doing again what had always defined him. Floyd Stokes was back at work.

AMAZING LOVE STORIES

BY DAVE ISAY
from *All There Is*

The Airport Connection

Lauren: I was 35 and living in Richmond, Virginia. Somehow a lifelong partner didn't seem to be in the cards; I was coming to peace with that. Then I bumped into an old friend at a conference. I started talking with him, but somebody else was standing there.

Stuart: I don't think you looked at me once during the whole conversation, but when you walked away, I said, "I have to meet her." Our friend said, "She usually goes to the afternoon social hours," so I showed up. And there I was, talking to you for the first time. There was this fascination with you that was almost magnetic. It felt like we'd known each other for a very, very long time.

Lauren: I was a bit dismayed to realize that you were living in Salt Lake City. There was the excitement of feeling really connected, but then we had to go our separate ways. So we began this long-distance thing: I was in Richmond, you were in Salt Lake, and our airline carrier was Delta. We'd fly through Cincinnati or Atlanta. Somebody—I think it was me, you think it was you—decided, wouldn't it be fun to leave notes for each other?

Stuart: We'd write a bit of poetry or some form of appreciation or just a thought. Then we would fold them up and tuck them under a chair in the airport and send a map to the other person with the gate area, and X marks the spot.

Lauren: Although we'd known each other for a only few months, it didn't seem right to spend Thanksgiving apart. It was a wonderful holiday. As I was heading from Salt Lake through Cincinnati, the only thing I could think to put on my note was "Will you marry me?" I wasn't ready to tell you about the note, but I was ready to write it. In March, I finally gave you a map to find the note.

Stuart: I flew to Cincinnati, and my plane was delayed in landing. I found myself running down the concourse, hoping to get to the next plane in time. I was running at a pretty good clip, and all of a sudden, I remembered the note. I was debating, should I stop and risk my connection? But I had to see if I could grab that note. So I peeled into the gate area and identified which chair it was. There was a fellow sitting there, wearing a very expensive suit, and I walked over and said, "Excuse me, I think I dropped my pen when I was sitting here previously," and I reached under the seat. I grabbed the note, took off running down the hallway, and got to the gate just before the door swung shut.

Lauren: Back in Richmond, I was thinking: Would you find the note? What were you going to think when you got it? I ducked out of a faculty meeting and drove out to the Richmond airport. I had a big bunch of flowers, and I felt like a bride waiting for her groom. I still remember you walking off the plane, and the minute I saw you, I knew you had found the note. You just had that glow. I had the bouquet of flowers, and we gave each other a big hug, and you said, "Yes!"

Recorded in Salt Lake City, Utah, on April 19, 2009.

Her Mother Was Right

Steven: The first time I met your mom was when she came up to me and said, "It's a pleasure to meet you. My name is Nadia, and I'm your future mother-in-law." The first words out of her mouth—I hadn't even met you!

Alexandra: My mom had been diagnosed with breast cancer in 2001. She had lost her health insurance and had to sell our house to pay for treatment. So she rented a house your dad owned. They found out that they both had single kids in their 20s, and they decided that we were perfect for each other. My mom invited you to dinner, and the second I found out about it, I said, "Call him up and disinvite him! You're not setting me up!"

Steven: I was pretty disappointed because my stepmother had showed me pictures of you, and I was like, "Wow, she's really cute! I would love to get to know her."

Alexandra: They had to find another way for us to meet. They were sneaky.

Steven: They concocted this story: My father wanted me to help him move stuff out of his rental property. So I was taking apart my sister's playground set that had been there for years upon years, and then your mother pulled up with you.

Alexandra: She got you to help her move, too, so we spent a week together—long, long hours.

Steven: You had invited your ex-boyfriend to come over. I remember you said, "Steve, you can go home. My mother doesn't need your help anymore, because my boyfriend's going to be here." But then your brother said, "Why don't you stay? My mother would really appreciate it." If I had gone home that day, I don't think I would have ever come back.

Alexandra: Seeing you and him together was important—how different you were. And then my brother said, "I think you're perfect for each other, and I don't think you're going to give this guy a chance." So I had to prove him wrong. By the end of the week, we were dating. Six months later, we were living together in New York.

Steven: Your mother passed away a couple of years later, and then my father had pancreatic cancer. I think it bonded us.

Alexandra: Today is our wedding day. We got married in City Hall.

Steven: I don't even think I said "I do." I said, "Of course I do! I'm the luckiest guy in the world." That's how I feel. I don't think I've ever been so certain about anything in my entire life, and I didn't hesitate a single moment. Before your mother passed away, I made a promise to her that I would always take care of you and love you. If you were ever in a similar situation with my father, what would you say to him?

Alexandra: I would tell him that I'm the luckiest girl in the world. I would never let you out of my grip. Ever.

Recorded in New York, New York, on July 18, 2008.

The Second Time's the Charm

Ron: Pepper would describe me as a ladies' man, and I was. Twenty-five years ago, I dated a lot of women, and most of the relationships were fairly shallow. But my conversations with you weren't shallow.

Pepper: I can't pinpoint when I fell in love with you, but I remember one time you left a message on the answering machine: "Hi, this is Ron. Just checking on you, baby." I absolutely loved that. I remember saving that message, and I would play it and play it. But when you first broached the subject of marriage, I was, like, "I can't marry you."

Ron: But I didn't quit.

Pepper: No, you didn't, thank God. We had a big wedding, and it was exciting. Walking down the aisle as Pepper Hunter and coming back down the aisle as Pepper Miller, that was a little startling. But I got into it; I enjoyed being Pepper Miller. We had a good life. But things changed, and I began to feel like our marriage was all about you, and I wanted it to be about me too. So we got divorced. It was painful. We went to the same church, and you sat on the other side. You dated people, and I dated people.

Ron: I poured myself into my work. But it was hard; I missed you.

Pepper: I missed you too. Remember when you called me and you had the flu? I came and made you soup. After tucking you in, I remember smelling your cologne on me. I missed the smell of your cologne. It's those little things that you miss. I would call my girlfriend and say, So-and-so is a really nice guy, and I have a good time with him, but . . . And my girlfriend said, "Well, the problem with this guy is he's not Ron, and the problem with the other guy is he's not Ron." I didn't want to believe that. Then my girlfriend said, "Don't hold Ron hostage to the past." When she said that, I started crying, and she's, like, "If you don't care about him, why are you crying?" Those words freed me to look at the possibility of us getting back together. I called you, and we started dating, and it was good. Then I took my dad on a cruise. We were unpacking on the ship, and in my suitcase there was this long letter from you, asking me to marry you. It was just a pouring out of your heart. That was in August. In December, we were married.

Ron: We were married eight years the first time, we were divorced five years, and this December it will be ten years we've been married again.

Pepper: We still have our bumps, huh?

Ron: Yeah. I guess we've learned that we're always going to have our bumps, but there's nobody that we'd rather be with. The lesson is to hang tough and make it work.

Pepper: And to be grateful. We have been through a lot together, but I'm still excited to be with you.

Recorded in Chicago, Illinois, on February 24, 2011.

Love at Long Last

Peter: I was at a skating rink one night when I was 16, in 1958, and I saw this young lady. I waited for you to take a break and get a Coke before I made my move. I grabbed you by the hand and said, "My name's Thomas Peter Headen." And you said, "My name's Jacqueline LeFever." I looked in those big green eyes, and it was a done deal. So we dated. Then, in 1959, your father got transferred to Japan. I decided, well, I'll go get her. I joined the Marine Corps, and I said, "I want to go to Japan." The Marine Corps said, "You'll go to Japan when we tell you you can go to Japan." So I went to a base in California.

Jacque: I dated a Marine while I was in Japan, and I ended up getting married—I guess just because I thought that's what I was supposed to do. We came back to the States in 1962, but I didn't know what happened to you.

Peter: Well, I finally got orders to Okinawa. And I said, Oh, boy. I'll go see Jacque when I get to Japan! I was home on leave—you always get leave before you go overseas—and stopped by to say hi to your mother. And she said right away, "Jacque got married. But here, you can have this picture of her." I made some excuse that I had an appointment or something— the walls were kind of crawling in on me—and I left. I went overseas for fourteen months, and then I came back to Camp Lejeune, North Carolina, not knowing you were right outside the gate of that base. I got discharged, and I went home to Maryland. One night the phone rang—it was you.

Jacque: I came to visit my mom. And I was calling your mother to see where you were, and you answered the phone—I was shocked, needless to say.

Peter: You said, "I want to show you something." We went to your mother's house, and here was this little baby. Your daughter was about three months old, and she had those same big green eyes. You went back to North Carolina, and I re-enlisted. That was 1964, and I said, "Send me overseas." I didn't want to be in North Carolina where you're sitting outside the gate. So I left on August 12 for Vietnam. I came back to the States after twenty-six months and was stationed at Camp Pendleton, California. One day I was sitting in the barracks, and I decided, I'm going to write her a letter and tell her how I feel, because we were going back to Vietnam.

Jacque: You wrote, "I just have to get this off my chest—I love you. I've always loved you. I have to say it and get it over with, and I'm done." In the meantime I'd had another child—a little boy. So there I was in an apartment with two little babies and just miserable, actually. I got married for all the wrong reasons. But I came from a divorced family, and I didn't want my kids to have a broken home.

Peter: When I came back from Vietnam, I spent 24 hours at home, and then I went to my mother at about 4 a.m. and said, "I've got to go to North Carolina." And she kind of looked at me: "I think you better leave that one alone—she's married. But I guess you got to do what you got to do." I said, "Yeah, I got to do what I got to do."

Jacque: I sent you away.

Peter: That was September 25, 1968.

Jacque: Thirty years after that, I left my husband. It wasn't easy. My kids were grown, they had their college education, they had their families, but I was lonesome and miserable.

Peter: I was sitting there one night, and the phone rang— matter of fact, it was September 25, 1998.

Jacque: That night, I had made up my mind: I am out of here. I'm so unhappy. And I sat there and I said, Nobody ever loved me but Peter. And that's when I thought, I'm going to go find him. I asked the operator, "Do you have a T. P. Headen in Waldorf?" And she said, "No." And I said, "Well, I'm really desperate to find this person. I know he's in Charles County, Maryland, somewhere." And she said, "I have a T. P. Headen in White Plains." So I said, "Oh, my God, that's it! That's him!" I started crying, and I said, "I have been trying to find this person for thirty years. He's the love of my life." And she said, "You want me to dial the number for you?" I said, "Yeah, you can dial the number." She said, "Can I stay on the line?" I said, "I don't care what you do!"

Peter: And you said, "You know who this is?" I said, "Yeah, I know exactly who this is." You said, "I bet you're mad at me." I said, "No. Matter of fact, I'm still in love with you."

Jacque: I felt like I was 15 all over again. We decided we would meet in Memphis, and I picked you up at the airport. You jumped in the car and gave me a big old kiss.

Peter: We got married in May, the 15th. I took you down to Key West and out on a three-masted schooner, and we married at sunset. There's no address on our marriage certificate, just a longitude and a latitude. It's worked out well. It's just sad, the time we lost—you can't get that back. We could have been together when we were 18, 19, you know? But I got you back. And you're just as beautiful as you were when you were 15.

Jacque: That's because you make me feel beautiful.

Recorded in Charlotte Hall, Maryland, on June 4, 2009.

Love Amid the Mortars

Joey: The first time we met, I stepped into your office and asked you to sign one of my papers—I guess it was for my meal card. But we didn't talk at all until we got deployed and I heard you were coming to Company B.

Delora: You sent me a couple of e-mails, but I was there to work. I was like, We're in Iraq. There's no time for romance. So we spent four months as friends, seeing each other at work. During that friendship phase, I heard you talking about your family, and I loved it. I'm very family oriented too. I also noticed your leadership—the way you talked to your soldiers and your supervisors, how you carried yourself, the way you dressed, how your weapon was always clean. I liked how driven you were. And as we became friends, I liked how you were opening up to me—you were so honest and real.

Joey: But you gave me the cold shoulder. So I was like, I'll stay focused on being friends for now. Because I knew one day you were going to change your mind.

Delora: The defining moment was when I was about to leave on R & R, but a sandstorm kept me in Baghdad. You were helping me with my bags outside the tent. All of a sudden we get indirect fire—mortars started falling. Boom! Boom! Boom! So I ran to the bunker. Eventually, you came in kind of casually, because you were seasoned. And then we were crouching across from each other, waiting for the all clear. I was just looking at you, and it was like a romantic movie scene where all the visions of the last four months come into play: Everything we talked about; how you talked to your kids on the phone; the fact that you called your mother; how you treated me. And I thought, You know what? I can't let this one go or I'm a fool. When I went on R & R, I had you on my mind. And when I got back, we would walk every night to get away from the other soldiers and talk. Doesn't really sound romantic, I guess: being fully dressed in uniform with a weapon slung on your back.

Joey: But from our perspective, we did what normal couples would do. We just did it in Iraq.

Delora: You picked out a ring online. And when you handed me the box, more mortars hit. We had to evacuate and go back into the bunkers. I thought, Is this a sign? Later that day, you walked me home.

Joey: That's when I got down on my knees with my weapon slung on my back, hoping we weren't going to get hit. And it wasn't your traditional engagement ring box—it was more like a post office box—and I tore that open and said, "Would you marry me?" I was kind of hesitant at first—being proposed to in Iraq is not what every girl dreams of.

Delora: But I knew you were the one for me. So when you said, "Do you want to wait?" I said, "No. This is where we are. This is the moment."

Joey: You didn't turn your back on me. You gave me a chance, and you accepted me. I can't ask for anything better than you.

Recorded in Frederick, Maryland, on May 22, 2010.

IN SICKNESS, IN HEALTH

BY SHARI LACY, AS TOLD TO ALANNA NASH

The year 1998 was the beginning of a remarkable transformation for my family. My father, Jim Dineen, the always healthy,
weightlifting, never-missed-a-day-of-work kind of dad, discovered he had kidney disease. He was 52, and had no symptoms.
We don't really know how he got it—he even guessed that ex-
posure to Agent Orange when he was in Vietnam could have
been a factor—and the road to recovery has been long. But in
November 2003, my father received a healthy kidney at Christ
Hospital in Cincinnati, where my parents live.

My mom, Joyce, a year his junior, was his donor. After years
of marital ups and downs, multiple surgeries for complications
of the disease, and financial challenges by the dozens, our family dynamic changed for all of us in ways we never could have
expected.

My parents have certainly had their troubles, and as their child
I'll never know how they made it to thirty-eight years of marriage.
They loved each other, but they didn't seem to like each other

very much. Dad was too fond of his beer, and he talked down to Mom a lot. When she tried to stand up to him, a fight would inevitably follow. I remember Mom once coming to visit my sister Leslie and me when we were both attending Miami University of Ohio. She told us she and Dad were splitting. But ultimately, our parents stayed together because of their faith. They believed somehow that God had a reason for them to remain married, and resigned themselves to sharing their lives, however imperfectly.

It was my dad's disease that began to change things. In the beginning of his illness, he went through hell. In 1999, his electrolytes plummeted so low as a result of diuretics he was taking that he passed out and fell in the bathtub, fracturing both elbows and several ribs and suffering a concussion. He had been put on the steroid prednisone, and initially gained forty pounds of fluid and almost lived in the bathroom. Dad was self-conscious about his appearance, waiting until night to go out for groceries, and even then using the drive-through lane. The only time he really appeared in public in two years was at a wedding. Dad wanted to be there so much that he was willing to risk ridicule. (The only clothes he had at home that would fit on his swollen body were a gray sweat suit and slippers.)

I don't know where he found the strength to go on. During it all, my mother stood by, sympathetic and helpful. She was at his side through six stomach surgeries and thirty-five more procedures to drain fluid that had collected in his abdomen from the prednisone. He and Mom had to work as a team just to get him through the day. The dialysis treatments, which began in 2001, first took place in a clinic, three days a week. Dad's arm turned black from the needles. It's no wonder Mom felt terrified when he was approved for at-home dialysis—putting the procedure, and his health, in their hands.

Still, she was adamant about not letting him go through it alone. Each night, just like a first officer with the captain of an airliner, Mom went over his checklist with him step by step. At one point when his muscles atrophied, perhaps as a result of the prednisone, she taught him how to walk again. The process seemed to go on and on, tying them both to the house and robbing them of so much freedom. The decision to go ahead with a transplant for my father was a long and arduous one, mostly because he had liver damage too. One physician's assistant told him, "According to your file, you're supposed to be dead." And for a while, doctors mistakenly thought that he would need not just a kidney transplant, but a liver transplant too.

Dad's future hung in limbo. When the donor testing process finally began in the spring of 2003, numerous people, including me, my uncle Tom, and my mom, came back as matches of varying degrees. But Mom was the one who insisted on going further. She said she wasn't scared, and it was the right thing to do. We all stepped back in amazement.

At last a date was chosen—November 11, 2003. All of a sudden, the only thing that seemed to matter to Dad was telling the world what a wonderful thing Mom was doing for him. A month before the surgery, he sent her birthday flowers with a note that read, "I love you and I love your kidney! Thank you!"

Financially, the disease was devastating to them. Because he was too sick to work, Dad lost his consulting business; throughout the same period, Mom was downsized from two different jobs. So for months they had no income and were in real danger of losing their house. My father had given up his leased car, and when Mom's stopped running, they had to somehow buy two cars, which was another big drain on their already taxed resources. So my sister and I were humbled and surprised when, shortly before his surgery day, Dad handed us a diamond pendant that we were to give to Mom after the operation. He'd squirreled away his spare dollars to buy it.

At the hospital on the day of the transplant, all our relatives and friends gathered in the waiting room and became embroiled in a mean euchre tournament. My family has always handled things with a lot of laughter, and even though we were all tense, everybody was taking bets on how long this "change of demeanor" would last in my parents.

We'd informed Dad that if he chose to act like a real pain on any particular day after the operation, he wasn't allowed to blame it on PMS just because he'd now have a female kidney!

The surgeries went well, and not long afterward, my sister and I were allowed to go in to visit. Dad was in a great deal of pain but, again, all he could talk about was Mom. Was she okay? How was she feeling? Then the nurses let us do something unorthodox. As they were wheeling Mom out of the recovery room, they rolled her into a separate alcove to visit Dad. It was surreal to see both our parents hooked up to IVs and machines and trying to talk to each other through tears.

The nurses allowed us to present the diamond pendant to Mom so that Dad could watch her open it. Everybody was crying, even the nurses. As I stood with digital camera in hand, I tried to keep the presence of mind to document the moment. My dad was having a hard time fighting back emotion, and suddenly my parents spontaneously reached out to hold each other's hands. In my nearly thirty-five years of existence, I'd never seen my parents do that, and I was spellbound. I snapped a picture and later rushed home to make sure I'd captured that enormous, life-defining moment. That photo of my parents' hands said everything. After so many years of discord, it was apparent to me that they finally understood how much each loved the other.

My father stopped drinking early in his disease, and he's started back to the health club again to improve his muscle tone. He's fascinated by how quickly he's recovered physically. But I have seen so many more profound changes. It's as if the transplant healed our whole family. There's definitely been a softening to Dad. He's mellowed, and he has more patience now. He's not condescending to my mother anymore. Mom, too, has loosened up, since she's not dealing with all that anger. There's a closeness that they didn't have before, and the experience has deepened their faith.

Mom says she can see God's hand in this all along the way. I live in Nashville, and when I talk with my parents on the phone now, I joke and say, "Who are you people? You're freaking me out!" Because at times they act like kids. They laugh more and complain less.

For Christmas, Leslie and I gave them two framed photos linked together by hooks. The top photo is of their clasped hands on their wedding day, August 7, 1965. Handwritten on the matting it says, "For better or worse, for richer or poorer." The second photo is of that day in the recovery room. Their hands are intertwined with hospital bands and IVs, and on the matting it says, "In sickness and in health, 'til death do us part."

THIS THING CALLED LOVE

BY MAUREEN MACKEY
AND BRIDGET NELSON MONROE

He Gave Her His Art

*George Aye, Designer, 32, and Sara Aye, Design Consultant, 29,
Chicago, Illinois*

He: It took about two months to plan my marriage proposal to
Sara, my girlfriend of three and a half years. We're both design-
ers, and I wanted it to be something that would slowly reveal
the words Will you marry me? When a coworker put me in
touch with the owner of an art gallery, I decided to stage a fake
art show.

First I created it all with 3-D software. Then I made the
letters for "Will you marry me?" out of foam core, using a laser
cutter. I broke them into even smaller shapes, so there were
about sixty pieces in all, and I stuck each one on its own piece
of aluminum siding. The idea was to have the pieces at different heights, arranged seemingly randomly around the room.
But if Sara stood in just one place, she could read my question.

I set up a video camera where Sara would be standing to make sure the letters lined up right; it took a full forty-hour workweek to arrange them. It was a nightmare! I really sweated. About a week before, I sent an e-mail to Sara and all our friends, saying, "There's an artist, Serge Gandaora, who's having a show on Friday called My Early Muir Owl." I played with words: Serge Gandaora was an anagram of "George and Sara," while My Early Muir Owl was a jumble of "Will you marry me?" The studio owner even enlisted an actor friend to play Serge during the show.

The day of the proposal, I texted a few friends, "This is a big day. I hope I don't screw up." I just wanted Sara to know how much I loved her.

She: At the gallery, after I'd chatted with people for a few minutes, George walked over and said, "My friend can introduce us to Serge." Serge said his artwork was "all about the intersection of text and space." I was thinking, I don't see any text. But just to be polite, I said, "Oh, wow, that's great!" Then Serge said, "If you look through these frames, you'll see the world differently."

Well, I saw these frames—like little rectangles—placed all around the room. I looked through one, but I just saw white pieces. Then George steered me toward a pair of frames, one at eye level and the other a couple of feet off the ground. The lower one was a vehicle for him to get on one knee! I looked through the frame, and after a second, I saw the word you. It was magical, appearing as if out of nowhere. I moved my head one degree and suddenly the whole thing just came together: Will you marry me?

The room had gone silent. Everybody was looking at me. I

turned and saw George on one knee and I started to freak out. He was holding a ring, looking at me like, Well . . . ?

And I said, "Of course I'll marry you!"

It was amazing. I was crying, and I kind of fell against the wall. I remember thinking that he didn't have to work so hard to persuade me. I would have said yes anyway!

They Spoke a Romance Language

Heather Pucheu, property clerk, 31, and Fabrice Pucheu, artist, 34, Spokane, Washington

She: In my high school French class, there was a pen pal requirement. The matchups were completely random. When Fabrice and I started writing to each other, I told him about school, and he told me about his life in Lèon, France, as a landscape artist. For the next eight years, we shared our lives on paper. We were able to be really honest and say things many people probably wouldn't say to each other—there were no appearances to keep up. Each letter brought us closer than we'd been before, but I never expected anything but friendship. During these years, I dated, got married, got divorced, and dated a bit more. I continued writing to Fabrice.

Then 9/11 happened. It made me understand how short life is and that it could be taken away at any second. Fabrice and I really bared our souls after that, although I think we didn't realize how much our relationship was changing.

When Fabrice came to visit in September 2002, I went to pick him up at the airport, saw him, and fell in love at first sight.

I know it sounds hokey, but you never think it will happen until it happens to you. I just knew I was going to marry him. I was so happy to finally meet the person I had gotten to know so well as a friend—we had all of that groundwork laid already.

It was an easy transition to romance. I spoke a little French, and Fabrice spoke some English. We went on long walks and started this wonderful new chapter in our lives.

Now Fabrice is the cook in our family; I haven't had to cook a single meal since we got married. His quiche Lorraine and paella are my favorites.

To this day, I still have all of Fabrice's letters.

He: It was wonderful finally meeting Heather after knowing her long distance for so long. I just knew she was the one. After I got my visa and put all the paperwork behind me, she and I settled in Spokane together.

I am still painting landscapes. When people tell me my artwork is beautiful, I do not question why. I know the reason: My wife inspires me.

They Gave Love a Whirl

Sheila Wilson, Air Force chaplain, 56, and Tony Carter, Army veteran, 52, Southern New Mexico

She: As a busy professional, I really didn't have time to meet men. I was in my 50s and had never married.

I'm a chaplain and an officer in the United States military, so I wanted to make sure the man was the same rank as I was.

I wanted him to be comfortable with me. I wanted someone to walk with me, not in front of me or behind me.

Out of nowhere, I found a website called faithmate.com. In August 2007, I put my profile on it. Tony and I started to look at each other online, and we began chatting. He had been in the service, including a four-year stint in field artillery. He was retired, which was a relief; if he'd still been on active duty, we would have had to stop immediately because of my rank. Later that month, Tony came to my church to hear me preach. What better place to meet someone than in a chapel?

After that, we had lunch and met again a few more times. Then we went to the Maryland State Fair together. We stopped at a booth where a rabbi was counseling couples, and the rabbi said to us, "How long have you two been married?" We looked at him like he was crazy.

Later we got on the carousel. As we were going around and around and up and down, Tony looked over at me and said, "Ms. Wilson?"

I said, "Yes, Mr. Carter?"

He said, "Will you marry me?"

I said, "Oh, sure, is this how our life is going to be? Going around in circles, going up and down all the time?" Then I said, "Yes."

I already had my wedding dress. I had bought it four years earlier. I just knew it was the dress I would be married in.

He: I wanted to ask Shelia to marry me, and the rabbi helped me get my nerve up. After Shelia said yes, she and I walked around the fairgrounds, smiling the whole time.

On the way home, we picked our wedding date. I didn't want to wait until spring, and she didn't want to get married in the cold weather. So we compromised on October 27. The church was filled.

I told Shelia, "It's a little late in life for us. We're both in our 50s." But I was so impressed with her. She talks more than I do, but deep down, she's really an introvert like me.

One thing she did tell me: "You were well worth the wait."

He Had Her Back

Sarah Peterson, actress, 60, and Dr. Sherwin B. Nuland, physician and author, 78, Milford, Connecticut

She: I was working as an actress with the American Shakespeare Theatre in Stratford, Connecticut, when I developed a painful carbuncle on my backside. I had to go to the emergency room after the show we were doing. The doctors performed minor surgery and referred me to a local practice for a follow-up.

The day of my appointment, I was feeling crummy. I was so sick from the infection that was coursing through my body, I wasn't even embarrassed by that point. All I could think was that I wanted to feel better. And I was lying on the exam table on my stomach, with a drape over me, when in walked this very handsome man.

The doctor and I started talking. As sick as I was, I thought, Oh, he's cute. And he has blue eyes. I had to keep going back to his office so that he could change the dressing on this boil and check its progress. Our relationship went from there.

To think that at first, I felt this wonderful man would be a good match for an older friend of mine!

He: While Sarah was lying in the exam room, she asked me about the Hippocratic oath that was hanging on the wall. She had taken classical Greek in college, she said, and she wondered about the translation. I thought, This is an unusual patient.

During the next visit, our conversation was even more interesting. I wasn't accustomed to complex discussions about literature, art, and science while I was working on a patient.

A few weeks later, I went with my two children to see Sarah's group perform *Romeo and Juliet*. Another night, I met Sarah after the show. We ended up talking through the night, until 8:30 the next morning.

But the truly transforming moment was when Sarah invited me to her home for dinner. It was a really lovely evening. When the time came for me to leave, I leaned over, kissed this beautiful woman on the forehead, and went to let myself out the door. But as I tried to make a smooth and dignified exit, the doorknob came off in my hand.

It was like a bad movie! No longer was I the avuncular, benevolent doctor—I was a human being. All the seriousness between us drained away, and I realized that I was falling very deeply and sincerely in love with Sarah.

When both my children insisted I marry her, I knew I couldn't live the rest of my life without her. We have been married for more than thirty years.

TO SERVE WITH LOVE

BY A. J. JACOBS
From *The Guinea Pig Diaries*

The most common theme of all the e-mails I get—with the possible exception of those from Canadians who are furious that I once misspelled Wayne Gretzky's name (who knew Canadians could get so worked up?)—is that my wife, Julie, is a saint.

Readers have said they're in awe of her for putting up with the beard I grew for my book on the Bible and the endless stream of facts about, say, China's opium wars during my year of reading the *Britannica,* and all the other nonsense that has come with my writing projects. Some people have even said I owe her something—precious stones, perhaps.

But others have said I need to pay Julie back by spending a month doing everything she says. As in, a month of foot massages and scrubbing dishes and watching Kate Hudson movies (if Julie actually liked Kate Hudson, which she doesn't).

I can't argue that Julie's a saint. But the experiment is . . .

Well, if I'm being honest, it's actually a pretty good idea.

It'll let me explore the tricky power dynamics of the modern American marriage.

So I decide to launch it.

When I tell Julie about Operation Ideal Husband (or Operation Whipped, as my friend John calls it), she jumps for joy. I don't mean metaphorically. She bounds around the living room on an invisible pogo stick, clapping her hands and saying, "Yay!"

Julie usually does wear the pants in our family, to use a clothing metaphor. But for one month, I will wash those pants and iron them. I'll be geisha-like in my obedience and think of nothing but her happiness. I will be an obedient 18th-century wife to my 21st-century wife.

First I ask Julie to tell me some things she wants from me during this month.

She begins to talk. It's a good thing I brought a notebook.

"Well, let's start with the bed," she says. "No forcing me to the edge of the bed with your six pillows. No waking me up when you come in at night using your BlackBerry as a flashlight. And no talking during movies. No looking over at me during sad parts to see if I'm crying."

I'm scribbling away, trying to keep up. It's kind of disturbing how easily this river of minor grievances flows out of Julie.

"No buying the first fruit you pick up at the grocery store," she continues. "No wasting food. If the boys"—we have three— "don't finish something, wrap it up and keep it for the next meal."

My wife is in the zone. I have pet peeves, too, but I don't usually recall them with such accuracy and speed.

"No making fun of my family," says Julie. "No complaining

about having to go to New Jersey on New Year's Eve. If I ask a simple question like 'Is the drugstore open on Sundays?' and you don't know the answer, try saying, 'I don't know.' Do not tell me, 'It is a mystery that humans have been pondering for centuries, but scientists and philosophers are no closer to an answer.'"

Okay. I can see how that might get old. Fair enough.

"Go to sleep at a decent hour so you're not a zombie in the morning," she adds without missing a beat. "No telling me when an attractive woman friends you on Facebook in a lame attempt to get me jealous. No putting things back in the fridge when there's a teensy bit left."

"Now wait a second," I interject. "You just said, 'Don't waste food.' I'm getting mixed messages here."

"It's a fine line, but I think you can figure it out."

I must have looked like I'd just gotten beaned by an Olympic shot put to the forehead, because suddenly Julie softens.

"I love you," she says.

"Noted," I say.

"Good morning, honey! You look terrific!" I say, really playing this up.

"Thanks, sweetie!" she responds.

Soon after these niceties, Julie assigns me my first chore of the day. "Can you think of a third gift we can give your father for his birthday?"

Three gifts? That's my initial reaction. My reflex is to make some clumsy remark like "So two gifts aren't enough? What was he, born in a manger?"

Instead I just say, "Sure."

This is something I notice throughout the day. Whenever Julie says something, my default setting is to argue with her. It's (usually) not overtly hostile bickering. It's just affectionate parrying. Verbal jujitsu.

I also know it's not good. You playfully bicker enough, and after a few years, it stops being playful.

I've got to reboot my brain. Marriage doesn't have to be boxing. Maybe it can be two people with badminton rackets trying to keep the birdie in the air.

So I spend the day trying to suppress my "me first" instincts. For every decision, I ask, What would Julie want?

Checking with my inner Julie every twenty seconds or so is exhausting, though. I start to cut the cantaloupe for my sons' breakfast and stop. Julie once complained that I cut cantaloupes all jaggedly, like a graph of the NASDAQ. I couldn't care less, but it matters to her. So I use a sharper knife and make a smooth and straight cut.

"Are you liking this?" I ask as she watches me.

"Loving it. And it's great for our marriage. Right?"

"Right!" I say.

And bite my tongue.

I reflect for a moment: If I'd tried this experiment a couple of hundred years ago, I'd have been breaking the law.

According to Stephanie Coontz in her fascinating book *Marriage, A History*, if the wife was the head of the household, the husband wasn't just an object of contempt—he was a criminal. "A husband could be fined or dunked in the village pond for not controlling his wife," she writes. In Colonial America, men sometimes "sued for slander if neighbors gossiped that a husband was allowing his wife to usurp his authority."

In the Middle Ages, rural villages had charming rituals for those who didn't discipline their wives: "A 'henpecked' man might be strapped to a cart or ridden around backward on a mule, to be booed and ridiculed for his inversion of the marital hierarchy."

Coontz makes clear that for most of history, marriage was wildly undemocratic. Husband and wife were like czar and peasant, chairman of the board and receptionist. In fact, wifely obedience was pretty much synonymous with marriage.

So I would have been seen as a traitor to my gender. I tell Julie about my research and read to her from a 1788 poem by the Scot Robert Burns called "The Henpecked Husband": "Curs'd be the man, the poorest wretch in life,/The crouching vassal to a tyrant wife!/Who has no will but by her high permission,/Who has not sixpence but in her possession."

"You're very lucky you weren't his wife," I say.

"Yes. Very lucky," Julie replies. "But you're not allowed to do that this month."

"Do what?"

"Compare yourself to other husbands," she says.

One of Julie's guidelines for Project Ideal Husband is, naturally, that I should buy her flowers. I object that we're in the middle of a fierce recession (I know, not very obedient of me). Flowers in New York are so expensive, I surmise, that they're kept hydrated with water drawn from the fjords of Norway by specially trained geologists.

"It doesn't have to be flowers," she says. "Any gifts will do."

I was a decent gift giver when we were dating. I gave books and soaps and cinnamon-scented candles. Then the presents trailed off. Maybe my gift-giving deficiency is genetic. My dad is still living down the gift he gave my mom for their first Valentine's Day—absolutely nothing.

So I start bringing Julie a gift a day. Mostly no-foam lattes. But also DVDs and soaps and books.

I start to plan the gifts days in advance. I look forward to seeing Julie smile when I plop them on her desk. I haven't gotten any "jumping for joy" outbursts from her again, but when I present her with the autobiography of Maureen McCormick, who played Marcia Brady on TV before a bout with drug addiction, she rubs her hands with glee.

Over the years, I've observed that behavior shapes thoughts.

My brain sees me giving a gift to Julie.

My brain concludes I must really love her.

I love her all the more.

Which means I'm happier in my relationship—if a bit poorer.

I've always chipped in and done my fair share of housework. But just to make sure I've got it covered, I ask Julie to list all the household chores she does.

"I clean up the kids' rooms," she says. "I set up playdates for our kids. I take them to their doctors' appointments. I pay the bills. I get baby gifts for our friends . . ."

If this were a movie, it would show the hands of a clock spinning around, maybe whole calendar days flipping by. It's a long freakin' list.

"I fill the liquid soap dispensers. I wash our place mats. I get new ink for the printer." On and on it goes. Finally, Julie pauses. "This exercise may cause a lot of trouble for you."

I've been thinking the same thing. She does chores I did not even realize existed.

"Let me do it all this month," I say.

"I can't let you do that," she says, envisioning, no doubt, the chaos that would descend in a matter of days.

Still, I give it a try.

The next morning, Julie says, "Okay, call the pediatrician and schedule the . . . You know what? I'll do it. It's faster."

This is the problem. Julie is just more competent at a lot of these tasks. Or all of them. She is the single-most-organized person in the world. My wife actually tabs and archives all her magazines.

Okay. I decide I can master this domestic stuff too. I decide the key is to be aggressive, or proactive, as they say in business meetings. I have to be an alpha househusband.

I find out about a great cable-TV drama airing in two weeks. I type an e-mail to Julie: "Should we record it?"

Before I press Send, I pause.

The "we" in that sentence? That's actually "Julie." The true meaning of my e-mail: "Julie, would you record it?"

I delete the e-mail. I schlep into the living room and program the TiVo myself.

Yeah, I know. I'm a hero. But there are dozens, hundreds, of little chores to be done. I'm overwhelmed. One day, I spend two hours writing and the remainder of the day reattaching knobs to cabinets and putting stray CDs into containers.

To paraphrase the title of a recent bestselling book about modern-day women, I don't know how in the world Julie does it.

The truth is, Julie is actually the sensible one in our marriage, the straight man to my wacky schemes. I probably overrepresent the conflict. Sure, fights happen in our life. But I don't write about the hours of peaceful, contented existence we share.

Yet at twenty days into the Month of Doing All She Says, the power seems to have gone to her head. Her requests are coming faster, more abruptly.

"Change the batteries in the kids' toys."

"Clean out the coffee machine."

She even snaps at me. Literally. One night, I ask her something while she's watching *Top Chef*, and she answers me with three snaps and a wave of the hand, which is sign language for "Get out of the room now."

She's also e-mailing me daily to-do lists. One item on today's list: "Put four Diet Cokes and four beers (any kind) in the refrigerator."

I write back: "Thanks for allowing me to choose the brand of beer! You clearly have faith in my judgment!"

"You're welcome!" There's a pause. Then she writes, "This is the best month of my life. Let me make the most of it!"

I'm making chicken piccata for Julie—chicken with lemon juice, olive oil, and white wine. When she hears the baffling sound of me pounding the chicken breasts with a rolling pin, Julie comes into the kitchen. She looks surprised. Then skeptical.

"Is this going to be more work for me?" she asks.

"That's what you say to me when I'm making you dinner?" I reply, appalled.

"You're right," she says immediately. "Thank you."

In cooking my dinner, there is no Mr. Mom wackiness like there was in the 1980s movie starring Michael Keaton. The rice pilaf doesn't explode all over the kitchen walls. The chicken breasts don't send us to the hospital with botulism.

I light the candles, pour the wine, serve the chicken.

"No napkin over your arm?" asks Julie playfully.

Aside from the napkin oversight, I'd go so far as to say that my dinner is actually romantic.

"If you cook for me every night, we could have sex every night," says my wife.

"I don't want to have sex every night," I reply.

"I thought all men did," she says.

"All men who are 17," I say.

One night near the end of the experiment, I am sitting at the computer when Julie walks in the front door.

"What time did the boys go to sleep?" she asks.

"Six-thirty. They were very tired."

"Are you serious? Six-thirty?"

I like the look that is now spreading all over her face. It is a look of . . . surprise. Respect.

Shortly after that, Julie says to me, "You know, I think we've cut the sass in our marriage by about thirty-five percent."

I agree with her. Since I have been saying nice things to her all month, she's been saying nice things to me. Sure, it took a while for things to change. And Julie did actually snap her fingers at me—that's true. But overall, we have moved into a vicious cycle of niceness.

Finally, Julie admits, "I think this has been one of the best months we've ever had." She adds, "I'd like to thank the readers who came up with this idea. Although I'm still angling for the Year of Giving My Wife Foot Massages as a follow-up."

And just like that, the experiment ends. My last task at the end of the month is to find all the missing pieces to the kids' board games, a massive operation that involves bookshelf moving and rug lifting.

In the end, I see that this has been good for us. We've each learned to appreciate the other more. I've also learned the fine art of refilling liquid soap bottles.

I've even continued filling them. This extension of my diligence as a househusband has earned me "a big gold star," as Julie puts it.

It's not always about the grand gestures, we both came to see, but rather the accumulation of little gestures. The little gestures are the ones that count. So a gift of a John Legend CD goes—almost—as far as a necklace on a birthday.

Recently, when one of my readers met Julie, he asked her, "Why on earth did you marry A.J.?"

And she answered, "Because he makes me laugh, he cares so deeply about me and our kids, and he makes my days interesting. He also makes a decent chicken piccata."

A CURIOUS LOVE STORY

BY JOSEPH P. BLANK

After the prayers of the minister, the ring of relatives and friends around the twin graves broke up, and the mourners walked slowly away. It was difficult to believe that it was only two days earlier that Kurt and Helga* had decided to drive to Erfurt in East Germany to buy black currant plants for their garden. They had left their 4-year-old daughter, Anna, with Kurt's younger brother, Martin. When their car blew a front tire and crashed into a concrete wall, the couple were killed instantly.

Beside the graves, Martin held the sobbing Anna in his arms. The child was frightened and unable to comprehend that she would never see her parents again. Martin stared at her delicate features, narrow face and tousled blond hair. She looked exactly like her mother at the age of four. Exactly. At that time, 26 years earlier, Martin had seen Helga only for a

---

* The names in this true story have been changed at the request of surviving family members.

few minutes, but he vividly remembered that dazed, exhausted expression on her face. . . .

Early June was still chilly along the northeast coast of Germany, just south of Denmark. Kurt, 14, and Martin, 12, had permission from their mother to play along a favorite beach, but had been told, "Don't do more than wade, because the water is still too cold." Martin was the more spontaneous and outgoing of the brothers. Kurt was serious, thoughtful, almost taciturn. The one emotion that he expressed without reserve was a compassion for living things in trouble. He was always bringing home a stray dog or an injured bird.

As the boys came to the beach, they saw three young girls waving their arms toward the water and crying. They were the children of Heinz Meier, owner of the biggest farm in the area. Out at sea, bobbing on the swells, was a small yellow rubber boat. In it, barely visible, was 4-year-old Helga Meier. The panic-stricken girls said that the dinghy had been pushed out to sea by the strong wind. Their 9-year-old brother had just left to find help.

Kurt said, "It's forty-five minutes to the village. By the time help gets here, she'll be halfway to Denmark." He took off his shirt, trousers and shoes, and told Martin, "Keep the girls calm." He dashed through the surf and dived into the sea.

Martin had a watch, and now he clocked his brother. It took Kurt thirty-two minutes to reach the boat. Martin saw him alternately pushing then pulling it toward shore—opposed by a stiff wind. The rescue seemed to take forever. Finally, after an hour and forty-four minutes, Kurt was close enough to shore to stand. Martin and the Meier girls splashed in to help. The oldest girl wrapped the frightened child in two sweaters and hurried from the beach. Help from the village had still not arrived.

Kurt collapsed face down on the sand. Martin rolled him over and rubbed him with a dry shirt. His skin was white, his lips were blue. After a few minutes, Kurt asked, "Where's the little girl?"

"They took her home. Are you all right?"

"I think so. I'll just lie here for a while."

On their slow walk home, Kurt told Martin of his ordeal. By the time he had reached the boat, Helga was in water up to her hips. He didn't climb into the boat for fear of sinking it. A cup attached to a light rope hung from the side; he untied it, then gave it to the child and told her to bail. Clutching the rope, Kurt tried to swim, but made little progress against the rough waves. He put the rope between his teeth and swam backward. When he tired, he swung behind the boat, held on, and kicked hard until he felt able to use his arms again for swimming.

All the while Kurt thought that he and the child would surely drown. But somewhere he found the strength to reach shore.

News of the heroic rescue spread through the village. As congratulations poured in, however, Kurt appeared more and more disconsolate. "He never said a word," recalls his older sister, Iris. "But I knew what was wrong. Old man Meier didn't thank him for saving his daughter. Helga's mother would have, but she was dying in a sanitarium.

"Meier was a hard man, and he never once gave a sign that he even knew Kurt existed. After about a week, Kurt seemed to get over his disappointment. He never again mentioned the rescue."

World War II was now at its height, and Kurt's family moved from their coastal village to Weimar, in the interior of Germany.

The years passed. Iris married. Martin married, too, and had two boys. Kurt became a schoolteacher and remained single. (Martin used to call him *Hagestolz,* or "confirmed bachelor.") He rarely dated or went dancing. His recreation was chess, and he became a top player in the coffeehouses of Weimar. He had a dry sense of humor and an almost cynical attitude, which Iris thought was a disguise to hide his sensitivity.

In 1962—twenty years to the summer after the rescue of Helga—Kurt's ailing mother decided to visit relatives in her old home village in what had now become West Germany. Because she was sick and over 65, the East German government granted Kurt a three-day pass to accompany her.

On his second day in the village, Kurt took a walk to the beach where he had rescued Helga. Sitting on a rock staring out to sea, he suddenly realized that he wasn't alone. A tanned, blond young woman with a slim, almost boyish figure was leaning against a nearby tree.

Quite uncharacteristically, Kurt walked over to her. Impulsively, he told her that he had grown up in the village and that this was his first visit in twenty years. They began walking along the beach, shoes in hand. "Look," Kurt said, "my mother is visiting relatives, and I'm bored. Let's go dancing tonight."

She smiled. "Why not?" she replied, almost aggressively. "My name is Helga Meier."

Kurt stopped short. "The little girl in the yellow boat! I'm Kurt."

Helga nodded. "I heard that you were in town. I've come down to the beach three times hoping that you would be here. I wanted to thank you." Her expression turned somber. "Don't call for me at the house. I'll meet you at the crossroads."

That evening, Kurt and Helga did no dancing. They talked. Helga was depressed. "I always wanted to thank you," she said. "But I've often wondered whether it might have been better if you hadn't rescued me that morning. I think Meier feels the same way. He believes that my mother was unfaithful. I don't look like his other children, and he has never behaved as if he were my father."

"The rest of the family have followed his lead and treat me like a servant. I do housework and farm-work. I get nothing for it, and Meier keeps telling me that I am illegitimate. I have no one."

Seething inside Kurt was a feeling that he had never before experienced. Holding her hands, he leaned toward Helga and kissed her. "I must leave tomorrow," he told her. "Come with me. Marry me."

She was startled. "But you've known me for only a few hours."

"I know you. I love you."

Then, in a low voice, Helga said, "I like you very much. I think I could love you, but I don't really know." She smiled at Kurt. "Yes, I will go with you. I risk nothing. It is you who are taking the risk."

The next morning, Kurt confronted Meier outside the front door of his big house. He introduced himself—the name rang no bell with Meier—and flatly told the glowering farmer that he was taking Helga to Weimar to marry her.

The news infuriated Meier, but Kurt was adamant. "You can't stop me. It's difficult to get a pass out of East Germany. I am taking Helga with me now."

Back in Weimar, an astonished Martin couldn't believe that Kurt—his quiet, cautious bachelor brother—had met, proposed to and actually carried off a young woman within twenty-four hours. "And what's even more unbelievable," Martin told his wife, "is that it's *this girl*."

Love was magic for Kurt. His reserve was replaced by spontaneity. He laughed freely. His sense of humor turned from the sardonic to the gentle.

Helga was slower to change. During the first few months she was shy, withdrawn.

Gradually, however, her fears and doubts evaporated. She smiled more—a slow, understanding smile that turned her from pretty to beautiful. The explanation for her change was simple: she had fallen in love with her husband. In two years Helga gave birth to Anna. Kurt was unabashedly proud of his wife and daughter.

The couple were rarely apart. Kurt stopped visiting the coffeehouses where the best chess players gathered; he didn't want to take time from his wife and daughter. He had always disliked working with soil, but when Helga decided to plant a large plot of land, he became an avid gardener and worked at her side. Amazed, Martin told his wife, "I've never seen love change a man so much."

Their love continued to grow. Martin could see it in the way they communicated with a mere touch or glance. Even on social occasions they always sat together. Kurt couldn't keep his eyes off his wife, and Martin once kidded him about it. "I like to watch her," Kurt admitted. "She moves so beautifully, so gracefully."

"Good Lord, you really are in love with your wife," Martin laughed.

Kurt gave his brother a big grin and said, "Forever."

Martin now recalls, "Those were Kurt's best years. And they were the happiest and merriest years for all of us. When Kurt and Helga left, they took a lot of that happiness and merriment with them."

One beautiful summer Sunday, a year before the accident, the two families were in the garden that Helga and Kurt had made. The wives were picking berries; the children were playing; Kurt and Martin sat in the shade of an old, twisted pine tree, relaxed and at peace. Kurt began talking: "You know, before Helga, I really wasn't dissatisfied with my life. I knew what I had, and that was fine with me. But I didn't know what I didn't have.

"Then Helga! She opened a new world for me. Maybe I did the same for her. She made me know what being alive is, what it means. Now I can't imagine myself without her."

He paused, the said, "Do you believe that some things in life are destined to be? Is it possible? Was it meant for me to save her twenty-five years ago—for myself?"

FAMILY TIES

RED DAD, BLUE SON

BY JOE HAGAN

Things were going great. On the last night of our family reunion two years ago, my 62-year-old father and I walked along a beach in South Carolina, glasses of wine in our hands, and soaked in the warm air, the full moon, and the gravity of the years. I'm my dad's first child and only son, now married with three kids, a career, and a mortgage. From the surf, we could both see his grandchildren silhouetted in the glowing windows of the rented beach house. The moment for a toast had arrived.

And that's when my dad started talking about the Tea Party.

Somewhere along the way, my dad had come to believe that trying to sell me on his conservative politics was the equivalent of bonding. His opining, however, has always had the same effect on me: My jaw clenches, my back stiffens, and the charge of political discord transforms the most beautiful moon on the East Coast into a naked lightbulb hanging in an interrogation room. Suddenly, I'm trapped with a right-wing pundit who happens to be my dad.

Ever since George W. Bush beat Al Gore in 2000, the chronic red-blue conflict in America hasn't just been a spectacle on cable news; it's invaded our family's phone calls, vacations, e-mails, text messages, Facebook posts. It nearly destroyed my relationship with my own father.

Our father-son differences date back to high school, when my dad, an officer in the U.S. Coast Guard, personally wrote the essay for my application to a military academy, which I passionately opposed with a declaration that I was a "nonconformist" meant for unconventional pursuits (i.e., tramping around like Jack Kerouac). But the arguments we'd had about politics in recent years had been of a different intensity altogether.

During phone calls and visits home, the day's news headlines were like a background hum growing louder and louder, overwhelming us. It would start innocently enough: My dad would coyly ask what I thought of, say, the latest skirmish over gay marriage. "It's certainly a complicated issue," I'd say, as if trying to tiptoe past a sleeping dragon.

Inside, however, I was roiling, considering some close friends who were gay and in committed relationships. Unable to resist, I'd throw out a line to bait him: Hey, isn't tolerance an option?

"I'm not a live-and-let-live guy," my dad would assert gruffly, now freed to unleash his own opinions. "I'm live-and-let-live within a certain set of moral values!"

Global warming, immigration, Iraq, Nancy Pelosi—it didn't matter the subject: Before long, we were both on our soapboxes, red-faced and yelling. Hang-ups were frequent. During week-end get-togethers, the simple act of rustling a newspaper to the op-ed page or clicking my tongue at FOX News was enough to send my dad skulking out of the room like a wounded animal. I'd sit on the couch, depressed and confused. My beleaguered mom was left to mediate, trying to cool everybody down so we could at least have dinner together.

In 2004, I had the bright idea of writing a book about the divisions between my father and me, how they related to the larger national political dialogue. I typed up a sample chapter for publishers, full of scenes from our lives. I made some oblique references about the book to my father, but he somehow came to believe that I was writing an homage to him in the spirit of the late Tim Russert's *Big Russ and Me.*

Far from it: I was painting him as a modern-day Archie Bunker, spewing harsh opinions from his recliner.

Not long after, while babysitting my nephew, Dad found a copy of my proposal on my sister's computer while checking his e-mail. My sister called me the next day, apologizing profusely for having left it open on her desktop but also warning me that things were about to blow up.

I didn't hear from Dad for several days, and every hour that passed became freighted with more dread. For a couple of days, I thought we'd never speak again. When we finally did, it was a tense, emotional conversation. His voice was shaking. How could you think these things about me? You think I'm some kind of bigot? An ignorant redneck?

I apologized profusely, nearly in tears.

Given the emotional opera of the election that year, the consequences of our differences felt more significant than ever. It pained me to hear him say that he thought the war in Iraq was justified, for instance, or that women didn't have the right to choose. In my insular New York world, friends whose parents shared their liberal political views talked about my father the Republican like he had an unfortunate medical condition.

Something had to change in our relationship. I decided it was me.

I forced myself to pay closer attention to my father's life. While he was occasionally bellicose in his rhetoric, in everyday life, he was a different person. Actually, he was probably the most open and tolerant person I knew, my supposedly tolerant friends included. He had a warm, southern hello for total strangers in my Brooklyn neighborhood, socialized with liberal retirees in his own North Carolina neighborhood, had a gay photographer friend in town with whom he traded camera tips, and spent every Wednesday delivering food to the housebound. It reminded me of the old adage: Liberals love humanity but dislike people; conservatives dislike humanity but love people.

Over time, my dad's tolerance went from a confounding outlier (he's a Republican, and he likes people!) to a more complex reality—and a personal challenge to my own biases. My dad forgave me for the things I wrote in the book proposal (the book was never published). It was a quiet and, to my mind, major act of love. If I couldn't look past my own politics and extend a hand to my father now, who was less tolerant, he or I? And how important to the future of the United States of America was my winning an argument over taxes and deficits with my dad anyway? It was the man I wanted to have a relationship with, not his political agenda.

Bridging the divide required time and patience from both of us. We slowly began to migrate our conversations to new subjects, carefully finding topics that didn't naturally lead us down the warpath: his interest in photography, the successes and trials of my sisters, home repair, raising children. It was awkward at first, but after a while, I began to look forward to talking about real estate values or the price of heating fuel. And when politics did crop up, as time went by, I noticed we both came to agree on something: that polarization, so corrosive to our own relationship, was corroding everything else as well. "I can't stand to watch the constant partisan bickering anymore," he told me recently.

So when that night on a South Carolina beach was threatened with a sudden squall of Rush Limbaugh, I took a deep breath and decided only to listen, not to fight. It's not that I agreed with him. But I knew what was in his heart, and it wasn't the Tea Party. Mid-sentence, my dad caught himself too. He took a deep breath, sighed. We both just listened to the surf, falling into a temporary spell. When we came to, we were standing in this glorious place, that moon overhead, the whole country at our backs. A father, a son, a real family—a better union.

THE POWER OF TATTOOS

BY LYNN SCHNURNBERGER
from *More*

For her high school graduation, my daughter, Alliana, didn't ask for a MacBook or even a car. She wanted us to get tattoos.

Alliana wasn't the kind of girl you'd imagine getting a tattoo. She wore hardly any makeup, and she hadn't yet had her first drink. She had the gift of keeping me current (she introduced me to YouTube), but now that she wanted to let some stranger drill five-inch-long, ink-filled oscillating needles under two layers of my skin, I had to demur.

"Mom, you already get Botox," said this child to whom I'd obviously disclosed too much information. "How much more could this hurt?"

A lot, since I'd read that tattoo artists don't use numbing cream, because it can smudge the ink. Alliana's uncle warned that the first tattoo is a gateway and that my daughter's lithe, lovely body would end up covered in jagged lightning bolts and God knows what else.

Alliana's tattoo campaign started just about the same time as what my family called "all of the business" with my mother—the macular degeneration, the diminishing weight (she was down to 82 pounds), and what the doctors said was her failure to thrive. I couldn't make my mother feel better. But because of her, I did know I had to make the most of being alive. And for that, Alliana was my ticket.

I followed Alliana to DareDevil Tattoo. Punk rock blared as we were ushered into the back room. An indomitable fashion publicist once told me about an evening she'd spent with a couple of beaus and the writer Dorothy Parker. "Someone suggested we get tattoos," she had said, pointing to a petite flower on the inside of her ankle. "It would have been impolite to refuse." I felt the same way. If your teenager wants you to do just about anything with her, you do it. Even if it involves burning flesh. "Just the teeniest, tiniest heart," I told DareDevil's co-owner Michelle. The needles pinched my shoulder blade, but Alliana held my hand, and by the time I felt really uncomfortable, it was over. Alliana's took almost 30 minutes, but she bore up well. Afterward we went to lunch, flushed and giddy with excitement. I checked my cell phone and saw that there were two messages from the nursing home, reminding me of what a luxurious—and temporary—respite our afternoon adventure had been. Weeks later, after Alliana left for college, I'd reach my hand back several times a day to touch my tiny tattooed heart. And I felt somehow comforted remembering what was on Alliana's shoulder—something symbolic of her sweet nature: the bluebird of happiness.

My mother's last year was painful and infantilizing. The woman she became in old age stood in tragic contrast to the lively redhead who'd raised me. She may have been brought up to believe tattoos were pretty much only for sailors, but she had her own way of standing out. And she knew that the most important mark you make is on the people you love.

If your teen wants you to do just about anything with her, you do it. Even if it involves burning flesh.

MARRIED AGAIN ...
WITH CHILDREN

BY WENDY SWALLOW
from *Washingtonian*

I'm standing in front of a mirror at home in a lacy silk dress, wondering why someone my age would ever walk down an aisle. I do not look like a bride, not at age 46. Instead, I look like someone's mom, and, in fact, I am. I'm the mom of those two teenagers behind me, dubiously eyeing this soft pink concoction.

"Aren't you supposed to wear white?" my younger son asks.

"White is for virgins," my older son says.

"Oh, jeez," says the other. "That's a problem."

That's me, the problem bride. Since announcing my engagement, I've stumbled across a minefield of social commentary on remarriage. Many of my single friends are envious, seeing it as a fairy tale ending. Others look at the two sets of teenage boys we hope to merge into one happy household and shake their heads. Instead of a fantasy, it's the Brady Bunch gone bad.

Indeed, roughly two out of three second marriages fail, and for families blending children, it's even higher. If someone told me I had cancer and those were my odds, I'd start writing my will. But then there are our parents, who are elated—relieved actually—at the thought of getting us back inside this maddening, wonderful and mysteriously strong institution. Married again, with someone to watch out for us.

Charlie proposed during a thunderstorm, on the couch where we first smooched. For years I'd reveled in the identity of a scrappy single mom. Now I'm going to be a wife again. Someone cared for. Not scrappy, but indulged. This is both unsettling and attractive.

Our engagement is a secret at first from the kids, but the planning machine starts rolling anyway—Will I sell my house? Will we renovate Charlie's? What about schools?—and within weeks I sink into irritability. Everything Charlie suggests makes me angry, and then I realize I'm mad at him for upsetting our lives. Months later my younger son will say, "He's a nice guy. Why did he ask you to marry him?"

What he means, when I tease this apart, is that no nice person would do this to us—ask us to give up our home, our neighborhood, our life. I try to explain this to Charlie: "I'm mad at you for wanting to marry me."

He looks at me, his worry lines deepening: "I'm trying to make you happy."

"I know," I say, "and it makes me mad as hell."

The night I tell my boys, they cry, they argue, they shake their heads. My younger son, citing his own deep distress, the chaos theory and how we've moved four times in nine years, finally says, "Why do we all have to live together?"

It's an interesting question. The point of the chaos theory, he says, is that you can't really control things, even with good planning. He knows this from reading *Jurassic Park*. As much as I hate to admit it, I think he's on to something. I lie awake at night, trying to plan meals and computer use and chores, and the image of dinosaurs crashing around a kitchen feels appropriate.

Charlie's family goes to bed late and sleeps in. We work on the Ben Franklin model: lights out at 10, up at 6:30. They are nutritionally pure, while our ice-cream habit recently morphed into a root-beer-float addiction.

"Don't you worry about the kids' teeth?" Charlie asks.

"Uh, yeah," I say, feeling defensive. "But don't you worry about your kids' sleep deprivation?"

We both fret about how to get four boys showered, breakfasted and out of the house before school. I have visions of towels assigned by color, matching toothbrushes and lockers in the kitchen, one for each boy. Charlie listens and says patiently, "We have to be careful with the kindergarten model. I think the boys will laugh at this."

Instead, the boys develop their own model for family harmony: Each kid gets a room of his own, equipped with a fridge, computer and TV. One son suggests a food allowance, "so we can go out and get our own meals."

"No," I tell them. "That's called college and you get to do that in a few years, but for now we're going to be a family. A family eats together and watches TV together."

"Okay," they say. "Who gets to hold the remote?"

At least they're trying. It's March, a few months before the wedding, and we've taught the kids to play Murder in the Dark, a game that involves cards and a murderer and bumping around in blackout conditions. It draws attention away from that tricky question about the remote. The renovation of Charlie's Victorian is under way, my house is on the market, and the school issue has been settled. Wedding plans are in place. Things are moving along nicely—yet I'm depressed.

For years I've had a sign in the kitchen that says "Ain't Nobody Happy If Mama Ain't Happy," and I believe that. My sons believe that. Now I'm afraid that I'm going to be unhappy, the one who cracks in all this testosterone-scented mess. We decide to see a psychiatrist.

"After all these years of counseling couples and of being married myself," he says, "I'm convinced that the single most important thing to making a marriage work is . . ." He pauses for dramatic effect. Charlie and I inch to the edge of our seats.

"Communication?" I ask.

"Well, all that stuff is important, but what it comes down to is—the ability to tolerate the neuroses of the other."

We look at each other. Nobody said it was going to be easy. Finally, within weeks of the wedding, I wander into a store that has dresses for me. Not too *jeune fille*, not too mother-of-the-bride. I find one that seems perfect for a garden wedding, a simple but elegant ivory linen sheath. It makes me happy. I find nice ties for the boys, order yellow boutonnieres. And when they all get dressed up and slick their hair back, they take my breath away.

Minutes before the service, a thunderstorm slices through the garden. Everybody dashes for the house, where we huddle for half an hour, listening to the rain. Soon it clears, and the birds start to sing. We go out into the garden, say our vows, promise the four children we'll build them a family life of tolerance and support, and—poof!—we are married. I know it won't always be easy—that our children will test our commitment, each other, and us. That there will be days I trip over too many sneakers left in the hallway.

But I also believe in unexpected blessings. When we told the boys we were getting married, and most of them were so distraught, Charlie's older son called and said, "Hey, I think this is great." That night his call was what pulled me through. We will all have our moments, moments of doubt and of believing, but so does every family. What feels wonderful is that we get to create them together. And if they fight over the remote? We'll just turn off the lights and play Murder in the Dark.

A LIFE FULLY LIVED

BY LYNN WALDSMITH

Anna Ling Pierce wrapped her arms around her two young sons, J.T. and Mike, as they watched a crowd of brightly clad runners warm up for the 1998 Boston Marathon. The sharp April wind stung Anna's cheeks as she glanced upward, a hint of a smile on her face. Somehow she knew John and Ali were with them. A TV reporter suddenly thrust a microphone in her face. "Mrs. Pierce, after going through such a horrible tragedy, how does it feel to see your husband's dream become a reality?"

A horrible tragedy. The phrase hung for a second in her mind, the memories still so fresh.

"Two years ago we were a family of five," she heard herself saying. "A year ago we were a family of four, then a family of three. How blessed we are today to number in the hundreds."

No, this is not a tragedy, she thought to herself. *This is a love story.*

The oldest of Anna and John Pierce's three children, Alison was a strikingly attractive girl with long jet-black hair and a contagious smile. A fiercely competitive hockey player, she loved nothing more than to skate with her younger brothers on Snow Pond at their home in Princeton, Mass. Twelve-year-old Ali pursued life with unbridled energy and an irreverent sense of humor she shared with her father.

The shock was therefore numbing when she was diagnosed with liver cancer on December 23, 1994. Even more so when doctors revealed that the cancer was life-threatening. But Ali's fighting spirit helped her beat the grim prognosis, just as it helped her endure the treatment that soon began.

"There is one good thing about chemotherapy," she would joke. "You can never have a bad hair day."

The chemo wound up shrinking Ali's tumors. By the time she finished the regimen in May 1995, the result was nearly miraculous. There was almost no sign of cancer, making it possible to remove the affected areas surgically. Ali returned to her eighth-grade class the following fall.

The turnabout left Anna and John feeling inexpressible relief. Yet as time went on, they could see that Ali's illness had changed her. One day Anna noticed her looking sad and asked what was wrong.

"My friends don't understand what life is about," Ali said quietly. "They're upset because some boy won't talk to them or they feel fat. They just don't get it, Mom."

Sometimes her new perspective led to remarks that startled her parents. On one occasion Ali said, "Cancer is the best thing I've ever gone through."

How can she say that? Anna thought, flabbergasted. Unfortunately, the young girl's reprieve was short-lived.

In December 1995 came the devastating news that Ali's cancer had returned. Realizing how precious every day now was, Anna suggested the family go on a Hawaiian vacation provided by the Make-A-Wish Foundation. But Ali said no. "I've traveled," she told her mother. "Let someone else have the chance to go."

John and Anna took Ali to various specialists, seeking any avenues to keep her alive. The young girl, meanwhile, seemed remarkably at peace with her fate. Never did she say "Why me?"

Instead, it was Anna who would break down. To comfort her mother, Ali would say, "It's okay. What is, is." Ali took her last breath on November 3, 1996. Only after her girl was gone did Anna learn that she had asked her friends to wear red, her favorite color, to her funeral. Numb with grief, Anna went out and bought a red dress. At the funeral, she was astonished. Everywhere she looked there was a sea of red.

Each morning after Ali's death the words reverberated in Anna's head without mercy. *Ali is gone.* She would get the boys ready for school, drive them to their hockey games, do the shopping—all in a fog. *I'll cry every day for the rest of my life,* Anna found herself thinking.

Though he continued to manage a Worcester brokerage firm, John was equally shattered by the loss of his daughter. Three weeks after the funeral, on Thanksgiving Day, he excused himself during their holiday dinner. Anna found him in Ali's room, weeping. She held him close and heard him say, "The best day of my life will be when I leave this world and join Ali."

"Soon enough one of us will be saying good-bye," she replied softly. "Let's not have any regrets. Don't let the boys see you like this."

They talked a while longer and agreed that they should strive to live life to its fullest in Ali's memory. John kept his word. Cancer had taken his daughter, but he would not let it destroy his family. Instead, he set out to create a legacy to Ali that would help other children battling cancer.

Through the University of Massachusetts Cancer Center he established the Ali Pierce Endowment Fund, which would support pediatric cancer care and research. An ex-marathoner, John recruited friends and colleagues to run with him in future Boston Marathons, each person securing money pledges from sponsors. They called themselves Ali's Army, and John vowed they would raise $500,000 over five years.

Anna wanted no part of it. She had always been self-conscious in public—even as a leader of her high school's pompom squad, she would beg another girl to give speeches for her in front of the student body. And she couldn't bear to revisit the cancer center where Ali had spent too much of her young life.

"Don't ask me to do anything," she told John. "This is your baby."

She did agree to attend a memorial for Ali at Notre Dame Academy in Worcester. On March 31, 1997—the day before Ali's 15th birthday—Anna brought red carnations to give to the girls in Ali's class, but she found she just couldn't do it. It was too hard to see the girls, so vibrant and full of life. She asked one of the teachers to hand them out for her and went home.

In October 1997, just eleven months after Ali's death, John and the rest of Ali's Army headed to Hollis, New Hampshire, to train for Boston by running a half-marathon. Anna, who had stayed home with the boys on the crisp Saturday afternoon, was impatient. Where was John? He said he'd be back for Mike's hockey game, which was to start shortly.

When the phone rang, she thought it was John calling to say he would meet them at the game. "Mrs. Pierce," said a nurse on the other end. "I'm sorry, but your husband has collapsed. You need to come right away." Anna gripped the phone tightly.

"What happened?"

"They're giving him CPR," the nurse replied. Anna could feel the blood pounding in her ears as she hung up the phone and called the boys into the kitchen.

"Listen to me," she told them. "Daddy's collapsed. He's at the hospital. But Daddy's so strong, and he loves you guys so much. He'll be all right."

The frightened boys didn't say anything at first. Then 12-year-old J.T. spoke up. "He'll be okay. God would never do two terrible things to us in a year."

Her anxiety mounting, Anna called the hospital back and was transferred to an emergency-room nurse.

"Look," Anna said. "We just lost our daughter. I need to know my husband is still alive."

"Just a minute," the nurse said and gave the phone to a doctor.

"Mrs. Pierce," he said, "there's no other way to tell you this. We tried everything, but we were not able to revive your husband."

Anna felt paralyzed. She had suffered the worst loss that she could possibly bear. And now this? How could she tell the boys? Still, she couldn't have them go to the hospital with false hope. She bent down and took a hand from each son.

"Daddy's gone," she said quietly. "He's with Ali."

J.T. broke free of her grip and ran out of the house, shrieking. Anna hugged Mike as tight as she could, then they both ran after J.T. When Anna caught up with the screaming child, she shook him and forced him to look into her eyes. Then she put her arms around both boys and said, "We're going to be all right. We will make it."

She said it again, louder. Then she was yelling it with all her might, partly to out-scream J.T. and partly to convince herself. "We will make it!"

Later, at the hospital, Anna stared in disbelief at her husband of twenty-one years. There he was, a fit, handsome 50-year-old—his body already cold. Anna felt a suffocating sorrow, but she kept thinking, *John is with Ali. How can I not be happy for him?*

In spite of her anguish she felt glimmers of an inexplicable calmness. Anna learned that John had collapsed of a massive heart attack just ten feet from the finish line. He was wearing a baseball cap that read "In Memory of Ali."

Anna decided that her husband's soul had crossed the finish line and just kept going. When Anna woke up the next morning, she felt the sun's warmth on her face. Looking through her window, she was struck by the brilliant fall colors before her. For the first time since the loss of Ali, she felt as though her life had a crystal-clear purpose. She had to raise her two boys. And she wanted to live for John and Ali by carrying on her husband's goal of raising money to support pediatric cancer research.

Anna had seen how cancer had given Ali deeper insight into life, and she had witnessed John's transformation into a selfless person who had given his life for their daughter. Now it was her turn to act.

She wrote a letter to John, which she read at his funeral, the first time that she had addressed a crowd in years.

"I will raise our sons to be like you. And I promise you I will carry on the work you have started with Ali's Army. But now we will call it Ali and Dad's Army. My sweet John, thank you for all you have given us."

Anna, who had not paid a bill or balanced a checkbook for 21 years, now plunged headfirst into leading the crusade for Ali and Dad's Army. At the time of John's death, the Army had raised about $10,000. Her husband's goal of $500,000 was light-years away.

With so much fund-raising still ahead, there was no choice for Anna but to overcome her awkwardness in front of people. Just days after John's funeral Anna was interviewed on the *Today* show. When she watched the program later, she was stunned to see herself speak so clearly and without hesitation. She knew the words had come naturally because she had spoken out of her deep love for John and Ali.

Besides serving as the spokeswoman for Ali and Dad's Army, Anna also worked tirelessly behind the scenes for each of the fund-raising events. Many times the boys stayed up late with her, sitting at the kitchen table stapling flyers. Before and after each race, Anna wrote heartfelt cards to each runner in Ali and Dad's Army.

Hockey games had been added as a fund-raising event, and to generate enough ticket sales, each game needed to be organized and publicized. So, among other tasks, Anna solicited ads for the game program from local businesses, an undertaking that forced her to retell her painful story again and again. But the effect of her direct and heartfelt plea was powerful. Anna's listeners were visibly moved, and they lent their support.

Once, Anna attended a memorial for parents who had lost children to cancer. Each parent spoke tearfully of the child that had died. "I had a son," or "I had a daughter," they would begin. When it was Anna's turn, she won admiration from the grief-stricken parents by saying, "I have a daughter named Ali. She left this earth, but she goes on, and I continue to celebrate her life."

Without fully realizing it, Anna had reached a turning point, steering herself and others away from their pain with her positive message. Now there were days when Anna didn't cry. Like the time she returned to Notre Dame Academy on Ali's 16th birthday with a bushel of roses. This time she handed a rose to each girl in Ali's class and thanked them. She was happy to see these girls with such bright futures. Ali, she knew, had become a part of them.

Finally, at a hockey game on November 18, 1998, between Ali and Dad's Army—comprising family friends and former coaches of Ali and her two brothers—and alumni of the Boston Bruins, the group reached that once-so-distant goal of $500,000. Instead of five years, John's dream had been realized in just thirteen months. The money has enabled the University of Massachusetts Cancer Center to fund pediatric cancer research programs and to provide alternative forms of therapy to children with cancer.

A VERY LUCKY DAUGHTER

BY SHARON LIAO
from *Washingtonian*

I should have been just another face in the hotel lobby in Zhangjiajie, a city in central China. But my words singled me out.

"*Yun dou*," I repeated to the clerk. Maybe he understood English: "Do you have a gym here?"

The clerk blinked, and then reached behind the counter and pulled out an iron. I smiled blankly. My brain rooted through my limited Chinese vocabulary. Just then my dad strolled up, his eyebrows arched in amused triangles.

"She wants to know where the gym is," he supplied in rapid Mandarin Chinese, his native language.

He turned to me and explained gently, "*Yun dong* is exercise, Sharon. *Yun dou* means iron."

I mumbled a sheepish apology to the laughing clerk and glanced at my dad. A look of recognition flashed through his eyes. We'd gone through this before. Only this time, the tables were turned. For the first time, I realized how my parents must have felt throughout their decades as American citizens.

When I was younger, I would try to imagine my parents growing up in China and Taiwan. But I could only envision them in the grainy black-and-white of their faded childhood pictures. Their childhood stories didn't match the people I knew. I couldn't picture my domestic mom, unsure of her halting English, studying international economics at a Taiwanese university. I laughed at the image of my stern father, an electrical engineer, chasing after chickens in his Chinese village. I related to my parents' pre-American lives as only a series of events, like facts for some history exam.

My dad fled to Taiwan in 1949 as a 14-year-old, after the Communists won the civil war. His father fought for the losing side, the Nationalists. My mom's father, a Nationalist navy captain, also retreated to Taiwan. My mom, who was born in Taiwan, grew up thinking that her family would eventually return to China, after the Nationalists reclaimed their homeland. But that didn't happen. As young adults, my parents moved to the United States to lead better lives. They did not step onto Chinese soil for more than fifty years.

Then their friends arranged a trip to China. And they asked me to join them on the six-city tour. There were plenty of reasons not to go. I'd recently graduated from college and was itching to move from North Carolina to Washington, D.C., and start my new job. I cringed when Mom described details of the trip, which sounded like something out of Chevy Chase's "family vacation" movies.

"Everyone wear bright pink or blue hat," she said excitedly. "So no one get lost. Such good idea, don't you think?"

"Uh, yeah, Mom," I replied, thankful she couldn't see my grimace over the phone.

I debated whether I could spend over thirty hours trapped on airplanes next to my parents, who shout stomach-sinking questions like "Sharon, need to go pee-pee?" in public places.

My list of why-nots was jampacked. And yet something inside—I could not explain what—urged me to go. When the plane jerked to a stop in Shanghai, our first destination, all of those reasons I decided to go materialized in the expressions on my parents' faces. My mom folded and unfolded her hands impatiently in her lap. I was surprised and slightly scared to see my stoic dad's eyes glimmering with emotion.

He slipped his hand, soft and spotted with age, in mine. "Last time I was here," he said, "my parents going from north to south, away from the Communists. So much bombing. A lot of people starving." He leaned close. "You very lucky, Sharon."

That was my dad's line. When I would whine as a child, my dad's response was inevitable: "Some people not lucky as you."

But I never cared about being lucky. I just wanted to be like the other American kids. My parents, however, intended me to become a model Chinese American. Starting when I was 6, they would drag me away from Saturday cartoons to a Chinese church. I would squirm in my seat while a teacher recited Chinese vocabulary. I dutifully recited my *bo po mo fos*—the ABCs of speaking Mandarin. But in my head, I rearranged the chalk marks that made up the characters into pictures of houses and trees.

When I turned 9, I declared I wasn't going to Chinese school anymore.

"This stinks," I yelled. "None of my friends have to go to extra school. Why do I have to go?"

"Because you Chinese," my mom replied coolly.

"Then I don't want to be Chinese," I shouted back. "It's not fair. I just want to be normal. Why can't you and Dad be like everybody else's parents? I wish I were somebody else's kid."

I waited for my mom to shout, but she just stared at me with tired eyes.

"If you don't want to go, don't have to," she said, turning away.

I wince now when I remember my behavior. I want to lecture who I was then: Don't yell at your parents because they're different, because that is who they are. Listen when they teach you Chinese, because that is who you are. But I can only rationalize why I pushed away my parents' culture.

I grew up in Raleigh, North Carolina, in the early 1980s, before it became the diverse, vibrant city it is today. In our suburban neighborhood, the Millers across the street were known as "the black couple," and my family was dubbed "that nice Asian family." In elementary school, I was one of two Asians in my grade. For the most part, I fit in with my peers. My friends and I wore the same brand of jeans and dried our hair into the same frazzled messes.

But there were daily reminders that I was different. The pork dumplings in my lunch. My reflection in the bathroom mirror. Where did I belong? I remember facing this question on an elementary-school standardized test. The directions said to fill in race. The four choices made a neat row of circles: "White," "Black," "American Indian," and "Other." I glanced at my best friend, Sara, darkening the "White" bubble. I contemplated my options. I wasn't black or American Indian. I didn't consider myself "Other."

Weren't Sara and I the same? I filled in the "White" bubble. After the test, the teacher shuffled through the answer sheets.

"Sharon," she said. "You've filled in 'White' for your race. You should have filled in 'Other.' "

Heat reddened my cheeks. "I know," I said.

How could I forget? Though my parents had lived in the United States for decades, they still led a Chinese life at home. They spoke to each other in Chinese and read a Taiwanese paper. Chinese food covered our dinner table. Breakfast consisted of watery rice with pickled vegetables and meat, or fried eggs with soy sauce. At dinner I would douse my rice with ketchup and remind my parents that Sara's family ate hamburgers.

I envied my friends' relationships with their parents. My friends didn't have to worry that their parents would embarrass them with questions like "Is this good price?" and "What's this meaning?" My friends' parents chatted easily with each other and our teachers. Their parents understood dating, and what it was like to grow up with the pressures of drinking, drugs and sex. My parents discussed only my grades, career and prospective salary.

My mom speaks English like I speak Chinese: slowly and punctuated by ums and ahs. When someone speaks English too rapidly, my mom's eyes cloud with confusion. I instantly recognize her I-don't-get-it look, and I know it's time to explain something. About a month before we left for China, I helped my mom return a purchase to Wal-Mart. The clerk rudely ignored my mom's slow English, speaking to me instead. Later my mom thanked me for my help.

"*Xie xie*, Sharon," she said, patting my shoulder. "I have good American daughter."

"It's nothing, Mom," I said.

In the airport before we departed for China, my parents' friends herded around me. "Your parents so proud of you," said one man. "Always talking about you."

His words surprised me. I felt like I barely spoke with my parents. Did they really know who I was?

Then another question, the one I always managed to skirt, surfaced in my conscience: Did I even come close to understanding them?

The tour was a seventeen-day whirlwind. We visited lakes laden with lotus flowers, snapped pictures of jagged mountains rising out of the Yellow River, and hiked up stone stairs to intricately painted temples. I saw rice paddies cut like square emeralds into the mountainside. I toured a factory where the employees spun silk into sheets of gloss. But the best part of the trip was watching my parents.

They carried themselves with an ease unfamiliar to me. They blended into the throngs of Chinese people instead of sticking out in the crowd. Their voices swelled with authority. My mom translated the tour guide's Chinese in her unwavering voice, whispering historical anecdotes she'd learned in school. Often during the tour, my own face resembled my mom's I-don't-get-it look. At meals, my parents answered my constant questions about each colorful bowl that would rotate by on the Lazy Susan.

My parents chuckled at my response when a waiter put a bowl of soup on our table. While the other diners shouted with excitement, I was horrified to see the remnants of a turtle floating in the clear yellow broth. My table cried in dismay when I let the soup circle past me.

"Strange," said one man, shaking his head. "Such good soup."

My experience in China pieced together the puzzle I knew as my parents. For the first time, I saw them in their entirety. I saw them in their culture, not in mine. I realized that many things I found embarrassing or frustrating about my parents were normal in China. I understood why my parents talked and acted the way they did—and why my dad constantly reminded me I was lucky.

As in most Third World nations, scenes of poverty offset China's exquisite beauty. It was hard for me to step off our air-conditioned tour bus into a crowd of dusty children clutching begging cups. At one point my dad informed me, "Our tour guide makes 12,000 yuan a year. Can you believe it?"

The guide, who was just out of college, earned less than 1500 U.S. dollars a year. I could be this girl, I thought. And then I wondered, What would I be like if I had grown up here? How very different I would be. Maybe more like my parents.

During the trip I befriended Rachel, the daughter of my parents' friends. She spoke flawless Chinese. My dad complimented Rachel's dad, Mr. Chow, "Your daughter speaks such good Chinese. You must be so proud."

I felt awkward standing there. In Chinese tradition, Mr. Chow was supposed to return the compliment heartily. Instead he slapped his hand on my dad's shoulder and started talking about the next tour stop. The interaction touched an insecurity. Wasn't I Chinese enough? Why did I feel like an impostor in Chinese skin?

A few days after "the iron incident," as my run-in with the hotel clerk became known in our tour group, my parents and I sat on a bench overlooking stone monoliths. "Too bad I don't speak fluent Chinese," I said. "I should have listened when you tried to teach me." I wanted to tell my parents that if I could go back in time, I would accept myself for who I was and them for who they were.

My dad looked at me with understanding. "It's okay," he said. "You learning it now." My mom smiled supportively. "Never too late," she said.

The trip to China changed my life. Now when I speak to my parents, there is a mutual understanding. Our conversations extend past questions about where they went to eat or how my job is going. I talk about my life. My parents talk about what they were doing when they were my age, and I can imagine them with crystal clarity, fresh young students at Taiwanese universities. And I realize my dad has been right about something all along: I am very lucky indeed.

FRIENDS
FOR LIFE

FRIENDS INTERRUPTED

BY JACQUELYN MITCHARD

If you have that one friend, you're rich. That one friend is different from all the others, dear as they may be.

I met Jeanine on my first day of high school, more than thirty-five years ago, at the age of 13. Painfully shy, I had signed up for student council because I thought it might save me from wandering around a huge high school shamefully alone. It was still early in the day. I'd already lost my new green trench coat and couldn't remember which building my locker was in. Standing there in the office, miserable, I wanted to vanish into the paneling.

I heard a girl's voice: "Do you have a lot of friends?"

When I saw her—tiny, delicate, with beautiful eyelashes—I smiled and answered, "Are you kidding? I'm the girl nobody knows."

"Well, I'm nobody," Jeanine said.

That was it. The two of us were instant friends.

For the next six years, Jeanine and I spent hours on the

phone each weekday and virtually every weekend night together. As boys came and went, we drowned our sorrows in
tomato soup. In my mother's old Chevy, we cruised the West
Side of Chicago. We sat on Al Capone's grave one Halloween night. Lying on blankets under the stars, we'd talk of our
dreams, pouring our hearts out.

Jeanine wanted to sing on the Broadway stage. I wanted to
write a novel. "Why not two? Why not five?" she pressed me.

As high school progressed, I became a student council officer
and made friends by the score. Jeanine? She preferred the side-
lines. She was like the angel in my pocket. I never forsook her,
never excluded her. Other friends could not understand our devotion, because we seemed like such opposites. But we weren't.

Neither of us got much attention at home. Jeanine's parents
worked long hours. Mine had other fish to fry, and those fish
swam at the bottom of a highball glass. I don't think my parents ever attended a single high school event of mine, though
my mother made sure I dressed well—she wanted me to be the
prettiest girl (and the thinnest).

Jeanine and I remained a sorority of two, and even college
didn't intervene. Neither did Jeanine's early unplanned moth-
erhood during our freshman year. After her daughter, Gemma,
was born, Jeanine moved back home. My mother, I'm proud to
say, offered them both love and support.

Unfortunately, Mama didn't get to play grandma for real.
After she was diagnosed with brain cancer and given just a few
months to live, I married a boy who was only a pal so she could
see me in a wedding gown. When my marriage was quietly an-
nulled, I came home for good, finishing school and working as

a waitress to help my younger brother get through high school.

Jeanine and I were together again, this time with a baby seat in the back of the car. We picked up where we left off, the Beach Boys on the radio as we cruised familiar routes.

Then, in my early 20s, I took a coveted job on a Wisconsin newspaper and had to start work every day at 5 a.m. Spent and challenged, I didn't get home often enough to see Jeanine through the terror she felt when her beloved father learned that he, too, had cancer. And when he died, I was too new at my job to take time off for his funeral.

The last words Jeanine spoke to me, for four years, were "You betrayed me."

I said thousands of words, through the crack under her apartment door, in letters, in cards, pleading with Jeanine to understand. But she was stubborn and wouldn't forgive me.

When I married for real, Jeanine was not there. When my beloved firstborn son arrived, she wasn't there to be his godmother, as I was to Gemma. And when my second and third sons were born after my struggles with infertility, Jeanine wasn't there either. But when cancer came to the door again, this time to claim my husband, Dan, Jeanine came, too, unbidden.

We didn't talk about the lapse in our friendship until much later. Suffering through hellish grief, I was simply staggered by gratitude. I kept thinking, *If Jeanine is with me, I can live through this. I can be okay. If Jeanine is holding me, helping me, I am home. I would never let her go again.*

We resumed our marathon phone sessions, dissecting jobs, life, her dates, my lack of them. When others called me foolish, she told me to go ahead, to write my first novel during the two years after Dan died instead of taking a real job. You can do this, she said. All I wanted was to show my sons that no matter the size of the hole life drove through you, you still had permission to live large.

In the end, my novel, *The Deep End of the Ocean*, became the first book ever chosen by Oprah's Book Club. Jeanine cheered—as she did two years later when I married my husband, Chris. And after Jeanine graduated from college with a degree in theater, I cheered for her as she became a sought-after voice and acting teacher, winning roles onstage and in commercials.

Before Jeanine even turned 40, her legs began to hurt. Deep into my aerobics period, I teased her: "It's because you're such a weenie." She wouldn't work out, but she did stretch, try massage therapy and take vitamins. Then an e-mail from a friend broke the news that Jeanine had been too devastated to speak: She had multiple sclerosis.

MS eats away at the myelin coating surrounding the nerves and can disturb balance, vision, and cognitive ability. People may end up using a wheelchair or remain mobile into their 90s. Although it affects more women than men, it typically affects women less seriously, so we didn't think it would be so bad. It was, though.

Jeanine was diagnosed with primary progressive MS, a rare form characterized by an almost continuous worsening of the disease, without relapses or remissions. Four years ago, I realized that my fierce, beloved friend, dedicated actress that she was, had never seen a Broadway show. Together we went—Jeanine pushing her walker, the two of us wearing our fanciest sequined skirts—to see her favorite musical, Man of La Mancha.

When Brian Stokes Mitchell sang of the impossible dream, the unbeatable foe, I had a brainstorm: I could use my small measure of new celebrity to raise money for something, and for someone. Jeanine had helped me craft the heroine of my sixth novel, *The Breakdown Lane*, a dancer who in one harrowing year loses her husband and develops MS. I would donate a portion of the book's sales, and go from there.

Last spring, at an MS fund-raiser in Washington, D.C., I was about to sign books when I heard the old Bill Withers song "Lean on Me." I looked up. There on the screen, larger than life, was a photo of me with my head leaning on Jeanine's shoulder.

The coordinator read a letter Jeanine had written: "Jackie was popular; I was the little caboose. But she chose me, included me, and when she learned I had MS, she jumped in to help me beat this disease. She's more than a friend. She's my heart."

That goes for me too. Jeanine has to lean on my arm when we walk. But I have to lean on her a hundred times a year, when I turn to her with problems no one else understands, problems no one else can see me through. As she describes them, they're like locational humor: To get it, you had to be there. She always was.

OFF A CLIFF!

BY JEFF RENNICKE

It was faint but unmistakable, a voice barely audible in the distance. At close to twenty-five hundred feet on the northeast face of Bellicose Peak, fifteen miles into Alaska's Chugach Mountains, climber Greg Nappi listened. He had expected his climbing partner, Joe Butler, to appear at any moment atop the one-hundred-and-fifty-foot wall of ice just below and join him on the push for the summit. But Butler had not appeared, and now Nappi heard a faraway call for help.

Many times in the past six years, Nappi and Butler had been roped together on steep rock faces from Alaska to Argentina, their lives in each other's hands, a deep trust building between them. They knew each other's strengths and fears, personalities and patterns. Butler was usually quiet on the mountain, calm and steady. So when Nappi heard the shouting a second time, he knew something was really wrong.

"I could tell it was Joe, but it was coming from farther away

than I was expecting," Nappi recalls. He strained to make out what Butler was shouting.

"Nappi," he thought he heard. And then, clearly: "I think I broke my leg."

Alaska is a landscape packed with rock and ice. Twelve of the highest mountains in the United States jut like exclamation points into the sky, and more than fifty thousand glaciers, some larger than Rhode Island, glisten like huge jewels.

Butler, 29, and Nappi, 25, had both grown up in the East— Butler in Georgia, Nappi in Pennsylvania—but during their college years, Alaska beckoned. They met when they both landed summer jobs guiding tourists on the Matanuska Glacier, and it wasn't long before they began climbing together. They had much in common, but there were differences too. Butler was the better ice climber, Nappi better on rock, Butler's methodical rhythm balancing Nappi's enthusiasm. "We meshed as a team," says Nappi.

Last April, they planned two weeks of climbing in the maze of peaks surrounding the Eklutna Glacier in Chugach State Park, a half-million-acre expanse outside Anchorage. With thousands of feet of vertical rock and ice, it was, as Butler says, "a good place to get lost in." A bonus was Serenity Falls Hut, a backcountry shelter at the end of a thirteen-mile ski trail. "We could climb all day and camp there at night," Butler says. "It was perfect."

Four days into their expedition, Butler and Nappi set out for Bellicose Peak. They left the hut around 6:30 a.m. and worked their way up a tight canyon to the toe of the glacier. There they turned west and began a one-thousand-foot ascent of a steep, snow-filled gorge, known as a couloir. On the way up, they encountered a one-hundred-and-fifty-foot cliff of sheer ice.

Nappi, who had broken the tip off his ice ax two days earlier, opted to skirt the ice wall by climbing a nearby snow slope. Should Butler do the same or tackle the cliff on his own? "We looked at the pitch of the cliff," Nappi says. "We both felt all right about Joe soloing it. I've seen him climb stuff like that dozens of times." The men would meet up again at the top of the pitch.

As Nappi moved away to begin his ascent on the snow, Butler started climbing. He made it over the steepest section and then decided to take a break. To give his calves a rest, he turned sideways and pressed all the points of his crampons into the ice, using two ice axes like walking sticks for support.

"Just that quickly, boom, I was sliding," Butler says. The pitch was pure ice, slick and hard. In a split second, he'd picked up speed, ice rushing by him. With only ten to twelve feet before the drop-off, he remembers thinking, "If you don't swing your ax into the ice, you've got no chance."

But there wasn't time. He shot over the edge, out of control. That's the last thing he remembers. "I blacked out," he says. He slammed into the snow one- hundred and fifty feet below and began to slide. When he regained consciousness, he was another seven hundred feet down the slope, injured and alone.

When Nappi reached the summit, his partner was nowhere in sight. Then came Butler's shouts.

"I knew I had to get down to him," Nappi recalls. Securing an anchor in the ice, he began rappelling down the same route Butler had been ascending. He couldn't see Butler, but scratches in the ice, gear strewn along the trail, and a depression in the snow that looked to be the size of a man's body made it clear what had happened. Nappi worked his way down the peak, wanting to move fast but knowing that one slip could send him falling, too, leaving both men without hope of help. Years of first aid and mountain rescue training raced through his mind.

"Joe was responsive and alert when I reached him," he says. A quick assessment showed that Butler had most likely broken his left femur and snapped his collarbone. With a fall of that distance, Nappi also couldn't rule out a head injury or internal bleeding. "I had to get him off the mountain," Nappi says, but help was hours away, and they were precariously perched on a forty-degree slope.

Nappi splinted the broken leg with a snow picket, an aluminum stake that climbers use as an anchor in deep snow. Now what? They both knew they would need a helicopter to get Butler out, but there was no way anyone could land on a slope that steep. Nappi tried sliding Butler. "We got only a few feet. Joe's leg kept catching in the snow, and it was just too painful for him." Nappi remembered a plastic sled back at the hut. It would take time to get it—precious time they might not have if Butler had internal injuries—but there was no other way.

"I'm going to have to leave you, Joe," he told Butler, using a backpack upslope as a barrier to protect him from "hang fire," small rock slides that often careen down slopes in melting snow. And then he turned away. I'd better pace myself, he thought. This isn't going to end soon. As he hurried toward the hut, he tried to keep his mind off the dangers. But then a gust of wind would slap him back to reality and his friend waiting for him up the mountain.

Two hours later, Nappi was back with the sled. He tied Butler on, and they tried again. With an ice ax jabbed into the snow above him to keep them both from falling down the slope, Nappi was able to lower the sled one arm's length at a time, working his way down the couloir and onto a flatter area. It was slow work. It took them several hours to reach the foot of the slope, and by then, the wind had picked up. Snowy gusts came roaring off the glacier and stung the two men like bullets. Even this far down off the mountain, Nappi knew Butler couldn't survive for long if he was exposed to the elements. Once again, Nappi returned to the hut, this time bringing back a floorless tent, a sleeping bag, water, and food. He made Butler eat and drink something and secured the tent with rocks. "I wanted to make sure that even in that wind, the tent wasn't going to leave the earth," Nappi says.

They both knew what had to happen next. "There was no getting help if Greg didn't leave," Butler says. When Nappi hesitated, Butler urged him on. "I gave him a hug, kissed him on the head, and told him to go," says Butler.

"I will do anything to get you help," Nappi replied. "I'll kick a door down if I have to." Butler smiled. He was sure that was true. And then his partner was gone.

Along the east side of Eklutna Lake, Nappi concentrated on keeping his legs moving—skiing when he could, taking his skis off when it got too rocky. Doubt plagued him with every step. "I kept second-guessing myself: Did I do the right thing moving him or leaving him there? Did I miss something in my assessment? What about frostbite and hypothermia?" He stopped once to rest. But then he looked back at the cold, dark canyon behind him, thought about his partner alone in the tent, and kept moving.

Back at the tent, Butler drifted in and out of sleep, forcing himself to eat and drink in case he lost consciousness later. "I figured there wasn't much chance they'd be getting a helicopter in here anytime soon in this weather, so I told myself I wouldn't start getting crazy until seventy-two hours had passed," he recalls. "I thought I could keep it together for that long."

Surprisingly, the pain in his leg was still manageable. "Maybe my thigh muscles were so strong from all the climbing that they kind of held the bone in place," he says. With gusts slamming snow crystals up under the tent flaps, he worried that the tent would be blown off him. "I was pretty much crystallized," Butler says. But all he could do was try to rest, save his strength, and wait for his friend to get the help he had promised.

Fifteen miles down the mountain, an exhausted Greg Nappi reached an empty ranger station. "I knocked. I yelled. And then I kicked." Seconds later, he was inside and on a phone dialing 911.

Park ranger Ian Thomas shot up in bed to answer the call at 4 a.m. in his Anchorage town house. A mountain climber himself, Thomas knows the park intimately and is friends with many of the climbers who use it. As soon as he heard there had been an accident in a popular ice-climbing area, he thought, Man, I hope it's not someone I know.

He met Alaska State Troopers helicopter pilot Mel Nading at the airport, and fifteen minutes later, they had landed at the Eklutna station. The moment Thomas saw Greg Nappi, whom he had known for years, his fears were confirmed. "When Ian recognized me," Nappi says, "his shoulders just slumped." Nappi delivered the news: It was Joe on the mountain.

Both men knew time was slipping away. Nappi quickly described where he had left Butler. The rescuers, including a paramedic who had driven in from the local fire department, climbed into the helicopter and were airborne.

As they flew, Thomas saw snow blowing off the canyon walls in slashes of white. Visibility was narrowing, but Nading, who helps rescue some 350 people every year, stayed steady at the controls. "He put us exactly where we needed to be," Thomas says.

But there was no movement from the tent. "My biggest concern at that point was not hearing anything from inside," Thomas says. "The way that Greg had described the fall, I was worried that Joe had internal injuries that would have done him in before we got there."

He called out, "Joe, it's Ian." There was a short pause and then a reply.

"Ian Thomas," Butler said, with great relief.

Butler was stabilized on a backboard and loaded into the helicopter, but he wasn't out of danger yet. Cold wind dropping down off the glacier picked up speed like an invisible avalanche. At the controls of the chopper, Nading monitored the situation warily. "The wind speed was bouncing between forty and fifty miles an hour," he says. "Taking off into gusts like that was going to make for a very special departure."

With the aircraft rocked by gusts, Nading lifted off and headed into the wind and toward the glacier's ice wall, hoping for enough lift to withstand the expected downdraft when he turned downslope. He held the position as long as he could and then, at the last instant, spun the craft in midair, tail to the wind. The helicopter rose up and out of the valley.

Within minutes, they landed at Providence Alaska Medical Center in Anchorage, where Butler's wife, Amara Liggett, waited. From the gurney, Butler looked at her and reached for her hand. "I got messed up," he said.

Liggett held his hand and started to cry. "Yeah, you did," she answered.

"That was probably the hardest part of the whole day for me," Nappi remembers, "seeing Joe with his wife in tears." Off the mountain after hours of physical and emotional distress and now knowing that his friend was safe, Nappi finally let his guard down. "I welled up pretty good at that point," he says.

Butler spent three days in the hospital, with his wife, climbing partner, and friends at his bedside almost every minute. The close-knit Alaskan climbing community came together to support Butler even when he was out of the hospital. "There was always someone there feeding me, helping me get around," Butler recalls. The owners of the Bear Tooth pub, a local hangout where Liggett works as a manager and server, collected donations and matched every one. They raised more than $5,000 for Butler, who faced huge medical bills without insurance.

Less than a year later, Butler is climbing mountains again, grateful for his partner's courage that day. "He knows I would do the same for him," he says.

Indeed, Nappi does know: "When you head into the mountains, you have to understand that this type of thing can happen," he says. "And if it does, the responsibility is all on your shoulders. It just so happens that this time, it was Joe who slipped, and it was my turn for the responsibility of the rescue. Next time, it could be the other way around."

As he recovers, Butler can look out the window of his Anchorage apartment and see the mountains of the Chugach range. He and Nappi already have their eye on another Alaskan adventure. It's a mountain called Awesome Peak.

A WINNING FRIENDSHIP

BY MOLLY O'NEILL

Jorge Posada sat in the hallway of a Manhattan hospital in August 2000, unaware of the usual hospital noises—the squeak of rubber-soled shoes against the polished floors, the announcements and pages, the rattle of gurneys being pushed into the pediatric surgery suite. His infant son had craniosynostosis—a congenital birth defect in which the skull fails to expand properly to accommodate a child's growing brain—and was about to undergo a corrective surgery.

After the seven-month-old was carried into the operating room by Posada's wife, Laura, the ballplayer sat, elbows to thighs, head in hands, staring down at his loafers in the terrible silence that occurs when your child's life hangs in the balance and there is nothing you can do.

It was early morning, and the silence, said the 34-year-old Yankees catcher, was unbearable. Only death could be this quiet, he thought.

But sometime after the surgery, on another day, he remem-

117

bers sensing a powerful, athletic body take the chair next to his, and like a shift in wind, the silence changed.

"Derek didn't say anything," said Posada of shortstop Derek Jeter, a teammate he has known since 1992 when they played minor-league ball in Greensboro, North Carolina. "That's the way it is with us. When you're in it together, you don't always need so many words."

In the five years since, young Jorge has undergone four additional major surgeries and is thriving. Posada spends hundreds of hours a year raising money for the foundation he created for the research and treatment of craniosynostosis. His closest teammates—Jeter, center fielder Bernie Williams and pitcher Mariano Rivera—have donated money and attended fund-raising events.

"My friends came together around little Jorge," said Posada. "I didn't have to ask."

The four superstar athletes are the only players remaining since the Yankees began their amazing ten-year run—seven wins in the American League Division Series, six League Championships and four World Series titles.

They have spent twenty-two hundred days working together, playing some fifteen hundred games and logging hundreds of thousands of miles on the team plane. As a group or in pairs, they have shared thousands of restaurant meals, and shopped together for clothes, cars, stainless steel barbecues and state-of-the-art in-home theater systems. They've exchanged investment tips, supported one another's charities, served in one another's weddings, made fun of one another and sat in hospitals during family emergencies.

With trading rampant and team alliances constantly shifting, this sort of continuity is unusual. In a deeply interdependent game, where a single error can mean that every player loses his post-season bonus, the fact that the friendship has survived each player's bobbles and slumps as well as the glory days is remarkable.

The four-way friendship began in 1994 when Posada, Rivera and Jeter were playing for the club's triple-A team in Columbus, Ohio. There was, initially, with Posada and Rivera, the natural connection that occurs between a pitcher and his catcher. There was also the matter of the movies.

Posada, a family man, and Rivera, who is deeply religious, were not into partying, and Jeter was too young to get into the bars, so they went to the movies.

"We've seen about a thousand movies together," said Jeter. "You don't spend that long sitting in a dark place with anybody you don't love."

By the 1995 post-season, "Jorgie," "Jeet" and "Mo" had been moved to the Bronx. There, watching the playoff series from the dugout, the friendship, said Jeter, "really jelled." Like soldiers after the war, the rookies exhaled.

Eleven years later, they are four—they hooked up with Williams along the way—and possibly facing their final year together, now that he'll be a free agent at the end of this season.

Their accord is powerful, constant, palpable. Even as their clubhouse filled with new additions at spring training this year, the four veterans remained anchors of the locker room, communicating with one another with just looks and nods. A glance from Jeter alerted Williams to the approach of an unfriendly reporter.

A look from Williams let the others know that several well-loved old-timers had entered the room. And when Rivera returned from the training room—his shoulder fat with ice packs and medical wraps—a simple nod from Posada asked the pitcher about the state of his arm.

When asked about their friendship, the players exchanged looks of alarm, followed by stares that dared the other to go first.

As effusive off the field as he is serious and contained on the mound, Rivera is the eternal jokester in the foursome, the clown who wears his feelings on his sleeve. "I love these guys," he said, his eyes narrowing slightly as they do in the moment before he releases his fastball. "They touch my heart deep. They make me better than I am."

His catcher is more circumspect. "Not many people have shared this sort of experience—the grit, the dream, the separateness," said Posada. "We spend more time with each other than we do with our families. You almost become close by default."

Neither this forced intimacy nor the bonds of accomplishment, wealth, prestige and history fully explain their friendship. "They share a turn of character that doesn't really have a name," said Joe Torre, the Yankees manager. "It's the same thing that tells me whether a guy will survive in New York City or crumble under the pressure."

Whatever that quality is, it yields big hearts and an awareness of one another that is deeply moving—and highly effective.

Last year, during the first game of the American League Championship Series, the guys rallied when Rivera returned to New York from the funeral of two family members who drowned in a tragic accident at Rivera's home in Panama. As soon as the pitcher appeared in the eighth inning, Jeter and Posada moved to the mound. In one of the most tender moments in baseball, Jeter's arm rested on the pitcher's shoulder, Posada gave him a gentle poke in the stomach, and far away, in center field, Bernie took several steps toward the infield.

The word *real* surfaces often, like a mantra, among these four friends. It is their highest compliment, and may be, said Williams, what keeps them connected to one another in the rarefied world they inhabit. "Some people get false with it," he said, opening his locker. "We stayed real."

A little later, Jeter watched Williams leave the clubhouse. Wearing a polo shirt, and sliding his cell phone into his jeans, the tall center fielder looked like just another guy at a suburban mall as he disappeared through the door.

"That was one of the first things I noticed about him," said Jeter. "You can tell by the way a guy carries himself if he is genuine or not." The reality factor, said the shortstop, is what initially attracted him to Posada and Rivera as well.

"Those first years are the loneliest," said Posada. "I came here from Puerto Rico. I didn't know a soul. I'd go home by myself. Once you sign up and go to the States, you are set apart from your friends at home. You think you are going to get new friends, but you find out you are competitors with your teammates and you don't know who to trust."

"I cried myself to sleep every night in the minor leagues," explained Rivera, returning to his locker from the training room. "I was so lonely. I couldn't even cry in English, man. Only Spanish."

Except for Jeter, who remains single, the four players all have family-oriented lives. "Winning draws you together too," said Williams. And their multimillion-dollar contracts are another common ground.

"Once you sign a big deal, your family and friends start calling you for money and stop talking to you about their lives," continued Williams. "They think they are protecting you, but it makes you feel like an outsider to your own life. We turned to each other more and more."

Bernie Williams is the older brother of the group. He is quiet and analytical. At spring training, straddling a chair in front of his locker, he leaned forward to talk, intently and eye to eye. A sense of finality lurks around the edges of his days. He is in the last year of a seven-year contract, and at 37, he keeps returning to what connects him to the players he is closest to, to the turn of character they share.

"So much of it has to do with fear and how you handle it," he said. "At first you are scared about not making it. The fear is selfish, and you use it to drive yourself. Then, after you make the club, you fear letting down the team and you use it to keep alert.

"Some guys get big behind the fear; they make themselves out to be more than they are. Other guys get gratitude. I've always stuck with the ones who know it's not them. We all know who we are, and we all know we're lucky."

Then, as if describing the final fear, the one that, traditionally, has bedeviled men, the fear of losing their purpose and their friends when they retire, Williams blurted: "I have no idea what's going to happen after the game. None. If I think about it, it takes my breath away."

As if sensing a shift in the emotional balance, Jeter glanced sideways from his locker. Across the clubhouse, Rivera craned his neck, and then he glanced at Posada. Posada shook his head.

Early in a player's career, fear is simply an energy, an itch. As a player matures, fear becomes a vision, a picture of one's final game.

"We say we will always be close. But you always think that every moment is always. And it never is," said Posada the next day, as the clouds vied with the sun to dominate the midmorning light. He joined Williams, Jeter and Rivera in front of the dugout for photographs, and continued. "I see how it is, once a guy leaves the game. We're all happy when he comes back, and there's a lot of catching up, and then there is this moment when there is nothing left to say."

A shadow passed over each of the four faces, and the camera began to *click, click, click.*

"Hey, man, we'll still be talking," said Rivera in his singsong English. He was seated in the center, and in his excitement, he let loose his arms, causing the players standing behind him to flinch and lose their well-practiced smiles. In that instant, affection and habit outweighed uncertainty. *Click, click.* The burst of laughter behind him was spontaneous, contagious—and real.

Earlier in the day, Rivera tried to capture the essence of this friendship. "I lost a lot when I got money," he said. "I lost a lot more when I got fame. As time went on, I needed these guys more and more. Other than my family and God, they are all I got that matters. The rest can go away in a minute."

Friendship. It doesn't get any more real than that.

FRIENDS FOR LIFE

BY ELLEN SHERMAN

The 77-year-old image is faded but familiar: forty-two third-graders from Cincinnati's North Avondale Elementary School. A small child in the third row stands out; John Leahr is the only black boy in the class. "Almost everything was segregated then," recalls Herb Heilbrun, an 84-year-old real estate broker, "so we didn't play together. I wasn't a racist, but I didn't have black friends. I just thought that's the way the world was supposed to be."

Little did Herb imagine that he and John would be inextricably linked for the next three-quarters of a century—that one of them would be instrumental in saving the other, and that a lesson in friendship would be taught.

More than a decade after the class picture was snapped, World War II broke out. The two men went their separate ways, never really knowing each other. Herb became a bomber pilot assigned to B-17 Flying Fortresses, and John, also wanting to do his part for his country, joined the Tuskegee Experiment.

ANIMALS
WE LOVE

PUPPY LOVE

BY MARY ROWLAND

Last Sunday our dog, Smudge, wandered off, probably into the 214-acre forest preserve on the edge of our property, a rocky, hilly patch of hundred-year-old oak trees where he once loved to run. My husband Bob, son Tom and I searched the forest, calling his name. No one knew how he'd make his way back. He's an old dog now, becoming increasingly blind.

That night, we got a soaking rain and the temperature dropped into the thirties. Did Smudge think his job with our family was finished? Had he wandered off to die? Smudge was gone.

We didn't tell our daughter, Krista, who'd headed back to college that same Sunday morning after yet another eye surgery, this time for glaucoma. She'd had a tough enough week already. After the operation, we made six trips to New York City, where her surgeon worked to stabilize her eye.

Between visits, Krista had commiserated with Smudge. The two of them, Krista with a patch of gauze taped over her eye and Smudge with hardly any sight at all, sat by the garden pond. He always knew when something was up with Krista, and he stuck with her while she cried about the pain and worried about finishing her art classes with just one eye.

Krista is 20, and a photography major. Strong and beautiful and resourceful. She believes the chronic troubles with her eye have helped her see in a different way, made her a better artist. I'm not sure how she might have turned out without Smudge. Not sure how I would have turned out either.

Like him or hate him (as Bob pretends to do), Smudge determined the arc of our family's life, helping Krista and Tom to grow more compassionate, Bob more tolerant, me more patient. Maybe even wiser.

Let's back up to an evening in February 1993, when our pleasant family life turned upside down. Krista, then 6, announced that something was wrong with her eye. Her pediatrician had seen no reason to worry when he'd examined her a few weeks earlier. But when we started making the rounds of the ophthalmologists, they all told us the same terrifying thing: Krista had no vision in her right eye.

Leukemia? Tumor? Lyme disease? No one really knew for sure. Sweat rolled down my back in the dead of winter while I tried to take this in and at the same time control the expression on my face so that Krista wouldn't know how scared I was.

Doctors suggested this was just the first shoe to drop. We'd have to wait. Would she be crippled? Would she die? At last, we found Michael Weiss, MD, an ophthalmic surgeon at Columbia-Presbyterian Hospital, who diagnosed uveitis, an inflammation in the inner eye that can destroy vision. He didn't know what had caused Krista's inflammation, but he warned that uveitis is often a harbinger of other autoimmune disorders. We were in for a rough ride.

Dr. Weiss first prescribed liquid prednisone, or steroids, in an attempt to reduce the inflammation. This worked, but only for a while. Next, he shot prednisone directly into Krista's eye with a needle, turning the eye blood red, hoping that the more localized treatment would douse the inflammation.

Of course, Krista was terrified. One morning when Dr. Weiss got out his needle, she fell apart, sobbing, and said, "I can't take it anymore."

Her vision was slowly improving, but the emotional toll was huge. She nearly doubled her weight, from sixty to one hundred and ten pounds. Wore my clothes to school. Went to a dress-up birthday party where she couldn't fit into any of the clothes the other kids were wearing. She was miserable and lonely, and she longed for a pet.

Bob said New York was no place for a dog. But every Sunday evening, Krista watched the TV show *That's My Dog*. Tom, the family's most fervent animal lover (his first word was dog), preferred *Beethoven*, a movie about a slobbering Saint Bernard that wandered into the life of a suburban family and ran amok. Eventually, Bob gave in.

We decided on an English Springer Spaniel. It wouldn't take up too much space and would be good with kids. Bob found a family in Connecticut with Springers, and we drove up to look at the puppies. The dog Krista and Tom picked was mostly brown, with just a smudge of white over his nose.

Before we brought him home, Bob said to me, "I don't like

the idea of a dog in the city. But whatever happens, I will never say 'I told you so.'"

Krista quickly became immersed in the dog world of New York, a new and secret place she could enter like Alice in Wonderland. We took Smudge to the dog park, a little fenced-in area where dogs could run. When we arrived, we would scan the dogs and tell one another who was there. Caspar, Nugget, Yank, Priscilla. Smudge loved Lucy, a more mature Springer.

We gossiped with the dog people about dog rules and which dogs misbehaved. We took Smudge to dog school, where he was the second most badly behaved dog. (One pit bull bit his owner.) Smudge wasn't mean. Just stubborn and adventurous. We didn't do a good job of training him.

On Saturday nights, Krista and Smudge and I camped out in sleeping bags in the room Bob and I used as an office. Smudge seemed to believe he was a dog king and we were his minions. He never listened to words like no! and stop! Pretended he didn't get it. Whenever Smudge misbehaved, Krista hugged him. Defended and protected him.

Perhaps Bob and I felt that leniency toward Smudge somehow translated into paying Krista back for some of her pain. Whatever it was, we didn't raise Smudge right. One friend said, "Your kids are so perfect. I'm glad Smudge brought some ruckus into your lives."

Or as Krista put it, "If we didn't have Smudge, we would be the boring family."

The big trouble started when Smudge was six months old and Bob and I took him out running along the East River. It was early March. Smudge chased a leaf that blew through the

"I'd always had dreams of flying, but there was no place for black pilots," John remembers.

In response to a lawsuit brought by a student petitioning to fly, a program to train black pilots was started. "The military thought they'd show we couldn't do it, and close it." But the Tuskegee Airmen surprised everyone, flying cover for hundreds of missions.

Still, it wouldn't be until 1995, when HBO produced a film about the unit, that the world would hear of the brave exploits of these pilots. The thrill of flying outweighed the disappointment John felt over the treatment he and his fellow airmen received.

"On our first day of training at Moton Field in Tuskegee," he remembers, "our officer said, 'You boys came down here to fly airplanes, not to change social policy. If anybody gives you a hard time off base, you're on your own. The Army isn't going to protect you; your life is in your hands.' "

White men in training to serve their country wouldn't be greeted so callously, John thought. "It was like he was saying, 'This is the South, and you're still black men. Your lives don't matter to anyone.' "

During the war, Herb flew thirty-five combat missions over Europe.

"Once, in December 1944, I was flying over Czechoslovakia," he recalls. "Eight hundred and fifty flak guns were aimed at us, and I was hit eighty-nine times. But I made it home because I had great cover from our planes."

Those planes were piloted by black airmen.

"Though the bases were segregated, we'd meet in the sky,"

John says. In more than two hundred escort missions, only about five bombers were lost to enemy fighters.

After the war, Herb returned to Cincinnati, married and started a family. He rarely thought about his time in battle. But one cold day in 1997, he read in the newspaper that his town was honoring the Tuskegee Airmen.

"I just wanted to give them a big hug for keeping those German fighter planes away from me," Herb explains. He headed over to the reception and began asking the men who'd gathered whether any of them might have flown at the same time he did. They pointed to a distinguished-looking man in the corner. It was John Leahr.

"This lanky, white fellow comes up and puts his arms around me," John recalls. "I didn't know what was going on." But after comparing mission books, John learned that he had actually flown cover for Herb on two missions in 1944. In fact, John's plane was among those that helped Herb make it home on that frightening December day.

"These guys were fighters, but they were told not to be aces—just protect the bombers at all costs," Herb says. "And they did. It was amazing to be able to thank him."

As John and Herb talked, they realized they'd worked at the same aeronautics plant before the war and at the same Air Force base after. John had gone on to become a stockbroker, but the two men had lived only minutes apart—a few miles from where they attended elementary school.

Herb went home after the reception and began looking for his old class photos. "I got out my third-grade picture, called John up and said, 'If this little black guy in the third row is you,

then this is getting really scary.' " Indeed, it was John, standing almost shoulder to shoulder with Herb.

The men began spending time together. Herb learned about John's homecoming after the war—so different from his own. While parades were given for white servicemen, John and his fellow airmen went uncelebrated. Sometimes they were even targets for scorn. Once, in Memphis with three fellow officers, John suffered a beating. "A guy came along," John remembers, "and said, 'I've killed niggers before, but I've never killed no nigger officers.' Two white policemen came up and just drove on. Luckily a sailor passed by and stopped the guy. If it wasn't for him, I'd be dead."

"If I had gotten killed," John told Herb, "not a thing would have been said. They would have just sent my body home. It was a terrible thought to have about the country that you'd been willing to die for."

But to counter any resentment he might feel toward whites after the war, John joined a multiracial church. "I couldn't go through life hating people just because of the color of their skin," he says. "I couldn't not forgive."

And through his wife, a teacher, he began giving talks at schools about his war-time experiences and the importance of overcoming prejudice. John invited Herb to come to one of his talks.

"I knew people faced racism," Herb admits, "but it never hit home until I heard John speak. And I felt a certain complicity. I hadn't done anything to make it worse, but I hadn't done anything to make it better."

When John asked Herb to join him at the lectern, Herb saw

it as a way to make good on a debt he owed to his new friend—and to hundreds like him, who'd been unsung heroes of the war.

"The kids are fascinated hearing John talk," Herb explains. "Then he introduces me. We give each other a hug. When we show them the picture of our class, they cheer."

In the fall of 2003, the pair received the Harvard Foundation medal for encouraging racial diversity. "Having Herb tell people how grateful and proud he is of us makes me realize I could have had this relationship for seventy-seven years, not just eight," says John. "Because of racism, he stayed in his world and I stayed in mine. We don't want that to happen to two other little boys."

"Adlai Stevenson once praised Eleanor Roosevelt because she'd rather 'light a candle than curse the darkness, and her glow has warmed the world,' " says Herb. "Johnny and I aren't about to warm the world, but I think our story has certainly lit a few candles."

BILL AND MARK:
A TALE OF TWO FRIENDS

BY ANNE FADIMAN
Condensed from *Life*

Bill Rush and Mark Dahmke are on their way to a University of
Nebraska football game. As usual, Mark, a senior in computer
science, is extremely well groomed; Bill, a junior majoring in
journalism, is a mess. His left arm is not all the way through
his down vest, and the bunched-up material makes him look
like a hunchback—one of the few things, as he would put it,
that he is not.

Bill's shoes are old and scuffed (though only on the sides—
the bottoms look brand-new). But the messiest part of his outfit
is the motorized wheelchair to which he is bound by four old
white bandages looped around his knees and ankles and tied
in bows to the battered chrome tubing. Bill is constantly doing
wheelies up curbs and kicking his footrests to pieces. He takes
the chair into the shop at the engineering college for repairs at
least once a month.

Mark is so quiet, so modest, so chary of unnecessary show
that next to Bill he is practically invisible. When Bill gets

excited he looks, as he says, "as if I am conducting 'The Flight of the Bumble Bee.'" He flaps his arms, bangs his feet, drools on his shirt and gets his hands stuck in peculiar positions that obscure his spelling board (a tray of letters and words placed across the arms of his wheelchair) until someone pushes them aside. When people hesitate to do so, fearing something will break, Bill spells out with his headstick (a foot-long copper pointer attached to his forehead): "D-O-N-T W-O-R-R-Y. I A-M Q-U-I-T-E D-U-R-A-B-L-E."

Mark's voice is low, carefully modulated and quick. When Bill, using his spelling board to communicate, spells something witty (which is often), he lets loose with a loud noise once described by his high-school teacher as "the mating call of a bull moose."

Bill Rush and Mark Dahmke also differ in their social habits. Bill tends to be surrounded by people whom he engages in relaxed and often sarcastic badinage. The part-time aides who bathe, dress and feed him say they hang out with Bill not because of their meager $3-an-hour wage, but because they find his conversation stimulating, because they enjoy his responses to their barrage of suggestions: that he pose for the centerfold of *Playgirl*; that he take singing lessons; that he cover himself and his wheelchair with a green poncho for a Halloween party and go as the Incredible Hulk. Bill is also fond of girls and has an active social life. Mark is by contrast a self-confessed loner. Late at night he is likely to be found in the computer center, staring at a simulated star map he spent many hours of his free time programming on an IBM computer.

Nevertheless, Bill and Mark have two important things in

common. The first is that they are smarter than most of the people around them. The second—though for Bill it is by accident and for Mark it is by choice—is that they are both outsiders on the Nebraska campus. At the football game they commit an act that brands them as visitors from another planet. When the Cornhusker star running-back scores his third touchdown, Marks says to Bill, "Want to leave?"

He leans over to read Bill's reply as seventy-six thousand Nebraska fans go wild.

"Y-E-S. T-H-I-S I-S I-N-C-R-E-D-I-B-L-Y B-O-R-I-N-G," says Bill.

Bill was born in Omaha by Caesarean section—after the umbilical cord slipped out of its normal position, impeding the flow of oxygen to his brain for nearly an hour. The obstetrician told Mrs. Rush that her son had cerebral palsy; that it was caused by damage to the portion of the cerebral cortex that controls voluntary movements; that it was neither fatal nor progressive; and that many children with cerebral palsy are also blind, deaf, or mentally retarded.

As Bill grew, the Rushes were certain that he could hear and see. They were also certain that he was not retarded, because his eyes followed them intelligently wherever they went. Bill's mother read to him often and was only mildly surprised when, at the age of 4, he had begun to read.

When Bill was 11, his teacher and therapists at the Dr. J. P. Lord School for the Orthopedically Handicapped started Bill on a regimen of neck exercises, made him a spelling board, found him an electric typewriter and presented him with his first headstick.

Before that time Bill remembers his life as a continuous series of temper tantrums: eleven years of physical therapy, steel leg braces and corrective surgery during which he never learned to walk; eleven years of speech therapy during which he never learned to talk; eleven years of occupational therapy during which he never learned to use his hands. The headstick was the first thing he had ever succeeded at. It was, he says, "like coming out of solitary confinement." He began devoting more and more time to his studies and eventually became J. P. Lord's first high school graduate. After passing his college boards (he typed the answers with his headstick), Bill entered the University of Nebraska at Lincoln, where he met Mark Dahmke.

Mark grew up in a small Nebraska town where he spent much of his time assembling electronic kits, watching *Lost in Space* and *Star Trek* and collecting science-fiction paperbacks. As a freshman in high school he entered a science fair. His first successful projects were a satellite with a proposed mission to the asteroid Ceres, a design for digital computer circuits, and an artificial arm inspired by his Uncle Armand, who is an amputee. The arm won first place in both the Greater Nebraska Science and Engineering Fair and the engineering division of the International Science and Engineering Fair.

After Mark received a scholarship to the university, he moved into Selleck Hall and later posted a card on his door that read: MCD CONSULTING, MARK DAHMKE, PRESIDENT.

MCD Consulting is an actual company whose president and sole employee has so far been offered six jobs in the microprocessor-computer field. Mark has turned them all down, largely because of a project that consumed all his free time for

four months and on which he still spends several hours a week.

In September 1978, $3000 was allocated to Mark by the Nebraska Division of Rehabilitation Services, United Cerebral Palsy of Nebraska and the university to design a voice syn-thesizer for Bill. Bill's spelling board is a surprisingly efficient means of communication, but he had always wanted to talk. So, to make the actual sounds of speech, Mark bought a $400 commercial synthesizer that produces a voice sounding rather like Wally Cox speaking with a Swedish accent. He adapted and hooked up the rest of the hardware: micro-computer, video display, disk drive, specially modified keyboard. That was the easy part. The programming to make the system useful for Bill took five hundred hours.

In February 1979 two of Bill's friends carried him and his wheelchair up the Selleck Hall stairs to the third floor—the first time Bill had seen Mark's room. Bill addressed his head-stick to the keyboard. The first sound it made was incompre-hensible. The second, in a Swedish accent, was "love."

The synthesizer, which Mark has christened the Bionic Voice and which now sits in Bill's room two floors below, has since branched out considerably in vocabulary. "O-N-E U-S-E-F-U-L F-E-A-T-U-R-E," explains Bill, "I-S T-H-A-T N-O-T A-L-L T-H-E W-O-R-D-S A-R-E N-I-C-E." If Bill wishes to say a word, he has several options. If it is one of the thirty-four frequently used words engraved on the keyboard (which include OOPS and HUH?), he merely presses the right key and out comes the word. If the word is not on the keyboard, the process is more complicated.

The computer cannot understand the vagaries of English

spelling, so a phonetic code with numerals indicating the degree of stress to be placed on vowels must be used. Since each symbol must be typed with a headstick, this is slow. Therefore, Mark and Bill programmed the Bionic Voice with a "dictionary" of 800 words and phrases chosen by Bill. The computer recognizes and pronounces these when Bill types their normal English spelling. They include: HELLO, THIS IS BILL RUSH; ARE YOU BUSY/ I NEED SOME INFORMATION; REHABILITATE, NOT SEGREGATE; HELP, SOMEBODY, ANYBODY; PLEASE DON'T BE AFRAID OF ME.

Mark is now working on a portable voice that Bill can carry around on his wheelchair. In the meantime Bill's telephone bills have skyrocketed. Over his touch-tone speakerphone Bill can for the first time in his life have a private phone conversation. And, while he originally requested a voice sounding like Elvis Presley's, Bill finds his new Scandinavian persona well suited for one of the final entries in his dictionary: WHAT ARE YOU DOING SATURDAY NIGHT?

Though the Bionic Voice has made their conversation easier, the relationship between Bill Rush and Mark Dahmke is based on deeper and more complicated levels of communication. "I once read a science-fiction story by Clifford Simak about two travelers from different planets who were so telepathic they shook minds instead of hands," Mark says. "Sometimes I almost feel that way with Bill. I knew Bill and I were really learning to communicate when I started having this dream. I'm just sitting around visiting with Bill. He's not using his spelling board. He's not using his electric typewriter. And he's not using the Bionic Voice. He's just talking."

guardrail and into the river, about eleven feet down from the walkway. Bob and I yelled, "No! Stop! No!" Smudge never hesitated.

We ran back and looked down at him, yelping for help in the water. Bob told me we had to forget about him. But I didn't hesitate much either. I climbed the rail and jumped in. With my shoes. I wasn't going to go home and tell Krista that I let her dog drown just as he was beginning to help her heal.

When I jumped, I sank down and down into the filthy river, never touching bottom, then floated slowly to the surface. A crowd gathered along the guardrail. A gymnast—I am not making this up—showed up and hung by his knees from the railing. Bob jumped in and lifted Smudge into the gymnast's arms. He couldn't reach me. A group of construction workers found a boat and got me safely to land.

In the ambulance, I felt so cold. My joints had frozen. My body temperature was 87 degrees, they told me at the hospital. I lay in the ER surrounded by big plastic bags of hot water while Bob went home for dry clothes. And Smudge, happy to be warm and dry, granted an interview to a TV crew in a room down the hall. He looked frisky and happy when we saw him on TV.

The reporter talked about how a woman had taken a death leap into the East River to save this little dog. The two of us shared the front page of the New York Post, him licking my face appreciatively, under the headline "Icy Plunge Saves Pooch."

Bob did not say "I told you so."

But Krista was improving. She carried a clipboard and wore a white jacket and pretended to be an eye doctor. Smudge was her patient.

"Can you see this? How about this?"

She marked down his answers on the clipboard. They dressed up in pink hats and purple dresses and went to the Easter parade. When Krista was invited to a sleepover, she called to talk to Smudge so he wouldn't be lonesome.

"What look does he have on his face?" she would ask after she'd finished talking to him.

Meanwhile, we continued to go to Dr. Weiss, sometimes two or three times a week when the inflammation flared up. Dr. Weiss said he really couldn't tell us what would happen. The disease was like the stock market, unpredictable.

Krista's vision deteriorated again, and Dr. Weiss suspected that a cataract caused by the uveitis had gotten worse. He removed the lens in her right eye, and she was fitted for a contact lens to replace it. She regained a good bit of vision, but the inflammation would often flare up under stress.

Bob and I are both self-employed. No benefits. Very high deductible on our health insurance. No coverage for prescriptions. A good way to save money, we once thought. Krista's prescriptions often cost over $100 each; they kept changing, so we had hundreds of dollars of leftover eyedrops sitting in the medicine cabinet. We felt as though we were shoveling money into a big furnace. But we didn't dare leave New York and relocate to a cheaper place. We needed Dr. Weiss.

Then, when Krista was 11, her eye seemed to stabilize. She very much wanted to live in the country, especially if it meant we could have more pets. So we took a chance and moved to the more affordable Hudson Valley. It would turn out to be a difficult transition for Krista. She couldn't fit in with the clique at her new school. She hated being "different" and calling attention to herself. Hated her round, chubby face and bloodshot eye. Grew terrified that she would never be able to make friends. The girls at the school made fun of her.

"Do you only have one pair of pants?" one asked.

Krista and I decided to shop for pants the next time we went to see Dr. Weiss. On our shopping trip, she stopped in the middle of a street in New York and said: "Are we shopping because I need pants or are we letting that girl tell us what to do?"

With only one pair of pants (mine), she clearly needed more. But she was developing a tough strength and wonderful values. Krista wanted to be an artist; her teachers in New York had praised her work. But there was one more obstacle: She was kicked out of the art program because her grade wasn't good enough. She dug in, took art lessons and signed up for a six-week summer course at the Rhode Island School of Design.

Krista wrote her college application essay about her eye, how she'd first discovered the problem. "One eye open. Shut that one. Open the other one. Shut that one because it doesn't work. Left eye. Right eye. Left eye. Right eye is the wrong eye."

By Krista's senior year of high school, Smudge and her summer art school experience had given her the confidence she needed. She could become an artist. She didn't have to believe the teachers at the high school who told her she wasn't talented.

She began to shop at thrift stores and buy wildly colored vintage clothes, and put patterns and colors together in a magnificent way.

When Smudge turned up missing that Sunday, the garden

pond was the first place we looked for him. He wasn't there. Five days after he disappeared, we got a call from the animal hospital. Smudge had been found that afternoon, caked with mud and burs, wandering down a road into a busy intersection two miles from our home. Bob went to pick him up.

I called Krista. "I'm so glad you didn't tell me when he was lost," she said. "I don't think I would have made it." The two of them had switched roles. Smudge was completely blind now and could no longer find his way. He was lost much too often and was miserable as a result. We knew he wouldn't be with us much longer.

More and more, Krista was moving out on her own. Camera in hand, she was following her own route to becoming an individual. And she earned straight A's, even in the wake of that last difficult operation. Soon she would travel to Venice for a special month-long photography seminar. Would we wait until she'd gone to Italy, she asked, before we put Smudge to sleep? She knew it had to be done but couldn't bear to be there with him when he went.

We did as she asked, and Smudge was put to rest in the spring of 2006. The dog who'd turned our lives upside down left us having put everything right.

MRS. DONOVAN'S DOG

BY JAMES HERRIOT
Condensed from *All Things Bright and Beautiful*

Mrs. Donovan was a woman who really got around. No matter what was going on there in our town in the Yorkshire Dales of northern England—weddings, funerals, sales—you'd find the dumpy little old widow, her darting, black-button eyes taking everything in. And always, on the end of a lead, her terrier dog.

I say "old," but she could have been anything between 55 and 75. She certainly had the vitality of a young woman, because she walked vast distances around Darrowby in her dedicated quest to keep abreast of events. Many people took an uncharitable view of this, but her acute curiosity took her into almost every channel of life in the town, including veterinary practice.

For Mrs. Donovan, among her other widely ranging interests, was an animal doctor. In fact, this facet of her life transcended all others. She could talk at length on the ailments of small animals, and she had a whole armory of remedies at her command—her two specialties being miracle-working condition powders and a shampoo of unprecedented value for improving dogs' coats. She had an uncanny ability to sniff out a sick animal, and it was not uncommon when I was on my rounds to find Mrs. Donovan's walnut, gypsy face poised intently over what I had thought was my patient while she administered one of her own patent nostrums.

"Young Mr. Herriot," she would confide to my clients, "is all right with cattle and such like, but he don't know nothing about dogs and cats."

And of course they believed her. She had the mystic appeal of the amateur, and on top of that she never charged for her advice and medicines. I often encountered her, and she always smiled at me sweetly and told me how she'd been sitting up all night with Mrs. So-and-So's dog that I'd been treating. She felt sure that she'd be able to pull it through.

There was no smile on her face, however, the day she rushed into the surgery and gasped, "Mr. Herriot! Can you come? My little dog's been run over! The wheel went right over him."

I was there within three minutes, but there was nothing I could do.

Mrs. Donovan sank to her knees. For a few moments she gently stroked the rough hair of the head and chest. "He's dead, isn't he?" she whispered at last.

"I'm afraid he is."

Later, she tried to smile. "Poor little Rex. I don't know what I'm going to do without him. We've traveled a few miles together, you know."

"Yes you have. He had a wonderful life, Mrs. Donovan. And let me give you a bit of advice: you must get another dog. You'd be lost without one."

She shook her head. "No, that little dog meant too much to me. I couldn't let another take his place. He's the last dog I'll ever have."

It must have been a month later when Inspector Halliday of the Royal Society for the Prevention of Cruelty to Animals rang me. "Mr. Herriot," he said, "I'd like you to come see an animal with me. Cruelty case." He gave me the name of a row of old cottages down by the river, and said he'd meet me there.

As I pulled up in the lane behind the houses, there was Halliday, smart and businesslike in his dark uniform. A few curious people were hanging around, and with a feeling of inevitability I recognized a gnome-like brown face. *Trust Mrs. Donovan*, I thought, *to be present at a time like this.*

Halliday and I went into a windowless, ramshackle shed. There was a big dog, sitting quietly, chained to a ring in the wall. I have seen some thin dogs, but this one's bones stood out with horrifying clarity. His hindquarters were a welter of pressure sores that had turned gangrenous. Strips of sloughing tissue hung down from them, and there were similar sores along the sternum and ribs. The coat, which seemed to be a dull yellow, was matted and caked with dirt.

"He's only about a year old," the inspector said. "And I understand he hasn't been out of here since he was an eight-week-old pup. Somebody in the lane heard a whimper or he'd never have been found."

I felt a sudden nausea which wasn't due to the smell in the shed. It was the thought of this patient animal sitting starved and forgotten in the darkness and filth for a year. Some dogs would have barked their heads off; some would have become terrified and vicious; yet I saw in this one's eyes only a calm trust. Here was the kind of dog that has complete faith in people and accepts all their actions without complaint.

"The owner's definitely simple," Halliday told me. "Lives with an aged mother who hardly knows what's going on either. It seems he threw in a bit of food when he felt like it, and that's about all he did."

I reached out and stroked the dog's head, and he immediately responded by resting a paw on my wrist. There was a pathetic dignity about the way he held himself—calm eyes regarding me, friendly and unafraid.

"I expect you'll want to put the poor thing out of his misery right away," Halliday said.

I continued to run my hand over the head and ears while I thought for a moment. "Yes, I suppose so. It's the kindest thing to do. Anyway, push the door wide open, will you, so I can get a proper look at him."

In the improved light I saw that he had perfect teeth and well-proportioned limbs. I put my stethoscope on his chest and, as I listened to the slow, strong thudding of the heart, the dog again put his paw on my hand.

"You know, Inspector, inside this bag of bones there's a lovely, healthy golden retriever. I wish there were some way of letting him out." As I spoke, I noticed a pair of black-pebble eyes peering intently at the dog from behind the inspector's back. Mrs. Donovan's curiosity had been too much for her. I continued conversationally as though I hadn't seen her.

"You know, what this dog needs first of all is a good shampoo—and then a long course of some really strong condition powders."

The inspector looked startled.

"But where are you going to find such things?" I went on. "Really powerful enough, I mean." I sighed and straightened up. "Ah, well, I suppose there's nothing else for it. I'd better put him to sleep. I'll get the things from my car."

When I got back to the shed, Mrs. Donovan was already examining the dog, despite the inspector's remonstrances.

"Look!" she said excitedly, pointing to a name roughly scratched on the collar. "His name's Roy. It's a bit like Rex, isn't it?" She stood silent for a moment, obviously in the grip of a deep emotion.

"Can I have 'im?" she burst out. "I can make him better, I know I can. Please, please let me have 'im!"

"It's up to the inspector," I said.

Halliday looked at her in bewilderment, then drew me to one side. "Mr. Herriot," he whispered, "I don't know what's going on here. But the poor dog's had one bad break already. This woman doesn't look a suitable person—"

I held up a hand. "Believe me, Inspector, if anybody in Darrowby can give this dog a new life, it's her."

Halliday still looked doubtful. "I don't get it. What was all that about him needing shampoos and condition powders?"

"Never mind. What he needs is lots of good grub, care and affection, and that's just what he'll get. You can take my word for it."

"All right," said Halliday. "You seem very sure."

I had never before been deliberately on the lookout for Mrs. Donovan, but now I anxiously scanned the streets of Darrowby for her day by day. I didn't like it when Gobber Newhouse got drunk and drove his bicycle determinedly through a barrier into a ten-foot sewer hole, and Mrs. Donovan was not among the crowd watching workmen and police get him out. When she was nowhere to be seen the night the fat in the fish-and-chip shop burst into flames, I became seriously worried.

Maybe I should have called round to see how she was getting on with that dog. I had dressed his sores before she took him away, but perhaps he had needed something more than that. And yet I had a lot of faith in Mrs. Donovan—far more than she had in me.

After three weeks, I was on the point of calling at her home. Then I noticed her stumping briskly along the far side of the marketplace, peering closely into every shop window exactly as before. But now she had a big yellow dog on the end of a lead.

When she saw me stop my car, she smiled impishly. I bent over Roy and examined him. He was still skinny, but he looked bright and happy; his wounds were healthy, and there was not a speck of dirt in his coat. As I straightened up, she seized my wrist in a grip of surprising strength and looked into my eyes.

"Now, Mr. Herriot," she said, "haven't I made a difference to this dog?"

"You've done wonders, Mrs. Donovan," I said. "You've been at him with that marvelous shampoo of yours, haven't you?"

She giggled and walked away, the big dog at her side.

Two months went by before I talked to her again. She passed by the surgery as I was coming down the steps, and again she grabbed my wrist.

"Mr. Herriot," she said, just as she had done before, "Haven't I made a difference to this dog?"

I looked down at Roy with something akin to awe. He had grown and filled out. His coat, no longer yellow but a rich gold, lay in luxuriant shining swaths over the well-fleshed ribs and back. His tail, beautifully fringed, fanned the air gently. He was now a golden retriever in full magnificence. As I stared at him, he reared up, plunked his forepaws on my chest and looked into my face, and in his eyes I read plainly the same calm affection and trust I had seen back in that black, smelly shed.

"Mrs. Donovan," I said softly, "he's the most beautiful dog in Yorkshire." Then, because I knew she was waiting for it. "It's those wonderful condition powders. Whatever do you put in them?"

"Ah, wouldn't you like to know!" She bridled and smiled up at me coquettishly.

A COP'S BEST FRIEND

BY MARK ROMAN

A fine time to have to break in a rookie, policeman Danny Miller thought as he cruised past the small office building on the outskirts of town. It was a bitter night in December 1988, just two months since he had been introduced to his new partner.

"Keep a sharp lookout," Miller told him, glancing toward the back seat. In the dim light, Miller could just make out the shield glimmering smartly from his partner's collar: Badge No. 85. The rookie was a husky German shepherd named Olden.

Suddenly the cruiser's headlights illuminated a figure breaking the lock on a building. Miller screeched to a halt and shouted the command "Go!" In a flash Olden bounded through the car's open window and was off, his deep bark reverberating through the night.

The chase ended seconds later as Olden nipped the suspect on the buttocks. Within moments, Miller arrived on a scene he will never forget: a trembling burglar standing at attention before a growling canine.

Back at the station, Miller felt a surge of pride as he came to the line marked "arresting officer" and typed "Badge 85." *Pretty good*, Miller mused. But as he reached down to give Olden a brief pat, he had a more somber thought: *Next time it might not be this easy.*

When Danny Miller joined the thirty-five-member force in 1978, Altus, Oklahoma, was a sleepy place where pickup trucks crowded the local shopping district and businessmen strolled the town square in cowboy boots. As the drug trade moved in, the number of crimes rose rapidly. Police Chief Jim Hughes had asked the city council for a larger force. In the spring of 1988, he broke the news to his department: The request had been approved—not for several more officers, but for police dogs.

The decision amazed no one more than Capt. Ron Myers, who well remembered the disastrous K-9 program Altus had tried 15 years earlier. Locally trained German shepherds had proved uncontrollable, attacking innocents without warning. Eventually, the program had been abandoned. *I wonder who the lucky cop will be*, Myers thought, shaking his head.

Chief Hughes chose Danny Miller, who he knew had worked for a dog trainer after serving in Vietnam. Miller was intrigued by the chance to handle such a powerful animal, but he also had misgivings. In a tough situation, could he trust the dog with his life?

That autumn, Miller stood in a parking lot waiting to meet his new partner. A van pulled up, and the biggest German shepherd he'd ever seen leaped from the back. *He's beautiful!* Miller thought, stroking the animal's coarse hair.

The dog, 2 years old and 110 pounds, was the product of fastidious breeding and training. Born near Reinheim, Germany, he came from twenty-five generations of German shepherds known for their strength, courage, good temper and intelligence. The canine left Germany with the highest level of "protection dog" training, *Schutzhund III*, able to obey dozens of commands. He could climb ladders, sprint forty miles an hour, sniff out narcotics, and take down a 270-pound man.

"His name's Olden," said Oscar Hall, the Tulsa trainer who had imported the dog. "Take him to live with you. Groom him. But remember, he's not a pet. You may have to send him to his death to save someone's life—maybe yours. So don't get too close.

As Miller drove home with Olden sitting calmly in the back seat, Hall's final words rang ominously in his ears: "Danny, it's better if you come back from work alone than if Olden does."

Over the next few months, Miller kept his relationship with Olden strictly professional. The dog was fed no table scraps. He was kept out of the bedroom. He spent his nights outside, regardless of the weather. Sometimes during storms, Olden would poke his nose out of his doghouse and bark at the back door. Miller pretended not to hear.

Day after day, Miller raced the dog around the back yard to build his stamina—after all, Olden was a soldier in training. To test Olden's discipline, he'd give him the order to "Stay"—and then he'd leave. Once Miller took a half-hour walk. When he returned, Olden was still glued to the spot where he had left him. At that moment Miller wanted to give Olden a hug, but instead quietly said, "Attaboy," and scratched him briefly behind the ears.

At the station, the other officers thought the latest addition to the force was a joke. They would elbow one another as Miller passed with Olden padding right behind. Myers saw only another catastrophe waiting to happen.

To Altus residents, however, Olden's massive black snout poking out the rear window of Miller's patrol car became a comforting sight. Shopkeepers slipped the police dog snacks. And Miller invited curious schoolchildren to stroke Olden's head and neck.

One night while patrolling a desolate street, Miller jumped from his squad car. Two burly drug users were swinging wildly at each other. As Miller struggled to pull the men apart, they turned on him. Dodging their blows, Miller felt a sudden alarm. Why did I leave Olden in the car?

Just then, a familiar bark shook the air. Olden had heard Miller's shouts and leaped from the cruiser's window. After a few deep growls from Olden, the two men backed away.

To respond to another call, Miller had to let his attackers run off. "They'll put the word out on the street about you," Miller said, patting Olden's head.

By the spring of 1989, Olden had racked up an impressive number of arrests. One afternoon, after a foot chase that spanned several city blocks, a burglar tossed a set of car keys into a vast, scrubby field. When the officers on the scene couldn't find the keys, they called in Olden. The dog zigzagged through the brush, then stopped short and pawed the ground. Officers found the keys lodged in the undergrowth and were then able to arrest the thief.

When a police call was triggered late one night by a silent alarm at the Altus High School, Olden tracked from room to shadowy room, with Miller following, hot on the intruder's trail. Moments later, Miller heard terrified screams as a thug, flushed by Olden, fled through a rear door to a nearby park. He ran straight into the arms of police officers, Olden snarling and snapping at his heels.

You're the best dog in the world, Miller thought. *I just wish I could let you know that.*

On May 21, just after Miller and Olden began their 6 p.m. shift, an urgent call came over the radio. "Shots fired, 720 North Park Avenue." Miller flicked on the siren.

As he pulled up to the house, a white car sped away. Behind the wheel was Steve Madden, a young hospital employee who had just shot his girlfriend to death.

Miller chased Madden through intersection after intersection at 90 m.p.h. Finally the suspect swerved down a side street and abandoned his car. Miller jumped out of his cruiser and raced past garbage cans into an alley.

Turning a corner, Miller expected to see a man running headlong for freedom. Instead, he found the barrel of a pistol pointing right at his chest. Miller was trapped.

He braced for the jolt as Madden squeezed the trigger. But suddenly a thundering bark rang out and Olden burst around the corner, tearing straight for Madden. The gunman fired and fled.

The bullet caught Olden in the face, spinning him backward and dropping him onto his side. The slug bore through

Olden's cheek, burst out his neck and buried itself in his shoulder. Blood spurted from the wounds.

It took a split second for Miller to react. *Olden has just made the ultimate sacrifice,* he thought. As his partner lay panting, Miller whispered, "It'll be all right." Then he went after Madden.

The suspect was now running across an open area behind a house. Officers Scott Young and Bob Carder had arrived, and the three cops exchanged shots with Madden. Finally, Miller felled Madden with a shot in the side.

Miller heard rustling from behind. He and the other officers watched in disbelief as Olden, dripping blood, staggered to the gunman and growled at him.

Miller scooped Olden up and placed him gently on the back seat of the patrol car. Then he sped toward the animal hospital, siren blaring, tears streaming down his cheeks. "Please don't die on me, buddy," he said.

At the hospital, as Olden was prepared for surgery, Miller was ushered out of the room. He feared he'd never see his brave partner again. Veterinarian Ronny Kiehn could promise nothing.

Back at the station, the mood was somber. Miller stayed there the rest of the night, mechanically answering questions from his superiors about the shooting. Occasionally a passing officer would put his hand on Miller's shoulder and say he wished Olden well. "We're pulling for him, Danny," Captain Myers said softly. "We all are."

At the hospital the next morning, Miller found Olden lying on a table, his shoulder and face shaved bare. Stitches jutted

from the closed wounds. "The bullet missed his jugular vein by a fraction of an inch," Kiehn said. "He's lucky to have made it this far, but he's not in the clear yet."

Miller stoked Olden's face and watched his eyes open slightly. The vet then dropped a piece of lead into Miller's palm. "You might want this," he said. Miller looked down at the bullet. *This was meant for me,* he thought.

As Miller began to walk out, Olden struggled to get up from the table and follow his master. But his torn body could barely move. "Danny, he wants to be with you," the vet said. "Take him home."

In the days that followed, Miller dressed the dog's wounds, made sure he ate and carried him outside. Soon it was clear to Miller that Olden was going to live.

His joy was tempered, though, when trainer Hall told him, "Gunshot wounds can destroy a police dog's effectiveness. He may be too gun-shy to be of use. If that happens, we'll have to remove him from police duty."

No! thought Miller. *He's my partner. He belongs here with me.* There was only one hope for keeping Olden on the force: The dog would have to pass a test to see if he could still perform his job.

Just weeks after the shooting, Miller drove Olden to an abandoned military base to re-create the scene of the shooting. Several officers stood by nervously.

Then Hall signaled the beginning of the test. Olden followed all orders, running down a long corridor and jumping out a window. But then an officer layered in padding dashed

out, leveling a .38 revolver. As Olden advanced, the officer fired twice close to the dog's face. Olden froze.

"C'mon, buddy," Miller said quietly. "Please do this for me." He re-commanded Olden to attack. A second later, the dog leaped at the gunman, now ignoring the gun in the officer's hand. The officers broke into applause. "Miller," Hall said, grinning, "you've got your partner back."

At home, Miller led Olden to his pen. Suddenly he stopped. There was something he'd been wanting to do ever since he saw Olden more than a year before. And now was the time to do it. Crouching down, Miller wrapped his arms around Olden and hugged him. Then the two started rolling around in the soft grass. Olden barked and barked, his tail thumping.

As the two romped, Miller heard Oscar Hall's warning: "It's better if you come back alone." Maybe so, Miller thought, but nothing beats coming back together.

SEMPER FIDO

BY LT. COL. JAY KOPELMAN, WITH MELINDA ROTH
From *From Baghdad, With Love*

I remember being exhausted. The tiredness weighed more heavily on me than my 60-pound rucksack. As I walked through the door of our command post in northwest Fallujah after four days of dodging sniper fire and sleeping on the ground, all I could think about was sleep.

That's when I first saw Lava.

A sudden flash of something rolled toward me out of nowhere, shooting so much adrenaline into my wiring that I jumped back and slammed into a wall. A ball of fur skidded across the floor, halted at my boots, and whirled in circles around me with the torque of a windup toy. Though I could see it was only a puppy, I reached for my rifle and yelled.

It was November 2004. In the days before our march into Fallujah, U.S. warplanes had pounded the Iraqi city with cannon fire, rockets and bombs. The bombardment was so spectacular that I—and the ten thousand other Marines waiting on the outskirts—doubted anyone would live through it. But

plenty managed. Now, sniper fire came from nowhere, like screams from ghosts.

At the sound of my voice, the puppy looked up at me, raised his tail and started growling this baby-dog version of "I am about to kick your butt." Then he let loose with tiny war cries—*roo-roo-roo-roo-rooo*—as he bounced up and down on stiff legs.

"Hey," I said, bending down. "Hey. Calm down."

There was fear in his eyes despite the bravado. As I held my hand out toward him, he stopped barking. He sniffed around a little, which surprised me until I noticed how filthy my hands were after almost a week of not washing. He was smelling dirt and death on my skin.

I leaned forward, but he tore off down the hall. "Hey, come back."

The puppy looked back at me, ears high, pink tongue hanging out sideways from his mouth. I realized he wanted me to chase him. He was giving me the "I was never afraid of you" routine. So I scooped up the little guy. He squirmed and lapped at my face, which was blackened from explosive residue, soot from bombed-out buildings, and dust from hitting the ground.

"Where'd you come from?" I said.

The puppy acted like he had just jumped out from under the Christmas tree, but meanwhile I called my cool to attention. *It's not allowed, Kopelman.* Marines letting down their guard and getting friendly with the locals—pretty girls, little kids, cute furry mammals—it wasn't allowed. But he kept squirming and wiggling, and I liked the way he felt in my hands. I liked not caring about getting home or staying alive, and not feeling warped as a human being because I was fighting in a war.

Born in Pittsburgh and a graduate of the University of Miami, I'd been a Marine since 1992, when I transferred from the Navy. Now, in my second deployment to Iraq, I was looking at a starving five-week-old outlaw. Members of the First Battalion, Third Marines—called the Lava Dogs for the jagged pumice they'd trained on back in Hawaii—said they'd found the pup at the compound when they stormed it about a week ago. He was still with them because they didn't know what else to do with him. Their choices were to put the little guy out on the street, execute him, or ignore him as he slowly died in the corner. The excuses they gave me were as follows: "Not me, man, no way." "Not worth the ammo."

"I ain't some kind of sicko, man."

In other words: Warriors, yes. Puppy killers, no.

They named him Lava. The newest grunt was treated for fleas with kerosene, dewormed with chewing tobacco, and pumped full of MREs. Officially called Meals Ready to Eat but unofficially called Meals Rejected by Everyone, MREs were tri-laminate pouches containing exactly 1,200 calories of food. Lava quickly learned how to tear open pouches that were designed to have a shelf life of three years and to withstand parachute drops of 1,250 feet or more.

The best part was how these Marines, these elite, well-oiled machines of war who in theory could kill another human being in a hundred unique ways, became mere mortals in the presence of a tiny mammal. I was shocked to hear a weird, misty tone in my fellow soldiers' voices, a weird, misty look in their eyes, and weird, misty words that ended with ee. "You're a brave little toughee. Are you our brave little toughee? You're a brave little toughee, yesssirree."

The Marines bragged about how he attacked their boots, slept in their helmets and gnawed on all the wires from journalists' satellite phones up on the roof. "Did anyone feed Lava this morning?" someone yelled out, as "I did" came back from every guy in the room.

He was always chasing something, chewing something, spinning head-on into something. He stalked shadows, dust balls and balled-up pieces of paper. He could drag a flak jacket all the way across the floor. But you couldn't yell at him. Even though you were an elite, well-oiled machine of war, you'd be considered a freak if you yelled at a puppy. So he was completely pampered and kept warm.

By the time I came around, he already knew the two most important rules of boot camp: You don't chew on bullets and you only pee outside. Lava gave the Marines something to be responsible for above and beyond protecting their country, and getting their brains blown out—or worse—in the process. He gave them a routine. And somehow, I became part of it.

Every morning we fed Lava and then piled out of the house to various posts across the city. Some Marines patrolled the streets; some cleared buildings looking for weapons; some got killed. Me, I supervised three wide-eyed Iraqi soldiers who, in their new, U.S.-issued, chocolate-chip cammies, waved their rifles around as if clearing away spider webs. They were untrained, out of shape and terrified, these members of the Iraqi Armed Forces, coaxed by the United States to help root out insurgents.

At night we all gathered back at the compound, where we covered the windows with blankets and sandbags, cleaned our weapons, and made sure Lava had dinner. After that, we would bed down and review the day's events.

"We found a weapons cache . . ."

"Yeah, well, we got caught in the alley . . ."

"Yeah, well, we had to transport wounded and then we got hit . . ."

As we talked, Lava would paw through our blankets. Then he would sit between my crossed legs and stare out at everyone.

As I untied my boots, Lava bit at the laces. As I pulled a boot off, he grabbed hold and tugged. I tugged back. The dog growled. I growled back. "Hey, what's with this puppy anyway?" I asked. "What are you guys planning on doing with him?" No one answered me.

Lava crawled out of my lap and turned a few circles, flopped down and fell asleep with his nose buried in my empty boot.

Like everything else in Fallujah then, nothing but the immediate was really worth thinking about. But when a puppy picked my boots to fall asleep in, I started wondering how he'd die. Especially when I knew I'd be leaving the compound soon and heading for Camp Fallujah about twelve miles away. In February, I'd be leaving Iraq for good and returning home to California.

I just knew the little guy was going to die. This one won't make it because he's too damned cute. As a lieutenant colonel, I also knew military rules as well as anyone, and every time I picked Lava up, they darted across my brain like flares:

Prohibited activities for service members under General Order 1-A included adopting as pets or mascots, caring for or feeding, any type of domestic or wild animals. The order was taken pretty seriously. The military didn't want anything like compassion messing things up. Our job was to shoot the enemy, period.

Most nights, Lava slept on the roof of the compound with a group of Marines, but once the weather turned colder, he came inside. He looked wide-eyed and cute, all paws, snuffles and innocence. In reality, he wasn't innocent at all. I personally saw the little monster destroy several maps, one cell phone, five pillows and some grunt's only pair of socks.

One morning I woke up and found Lava sitting near my sleeping bag, staring at me, his left ear flapped forward and the remains of a toothpaste tube stuffed in his mouth. "Morning," I said. He replied with a minty belch.

Another time, I woke up to see his entire front end stuffed into one of my boots, his butt and back legs draped out over the side. He wasn't moving. I thought he was dead—probably from all those MREs. "Oh, no," I said, cursing. But when he heard my voice, his tail started wagging like a wind-kissed flag. I decided that from then on, he wasn't eating noodles, biscuits or beans in butter sauce. No more toothpaste. Only meat.

And then another morning, I thought someone had short-sheeted my sleeping bag because I couldn't push my feet to the end. It was Lava, who'd managed to crawl in during the night and curl up at the bottom in a ball.

I pulled the dog up under my chin. He snorted and snuffled, and I scratched his ears. "What's going to happen to you once we leave here, little guy?"

The puppy thumped his tail on my chest. I realized that I could no longer sleep at night unless some little fur ball was nestled up against me. Though from day one Lava had been a group project, I was now considering him my own. I made his safety and well-being my mission.

I started calling friends and family, telling them about Lava and asking for help. At first I thought that the silences on the other end were the usual international lags on a cell-phone call. But I soon realized that my friends back home were trying to place the word puppy in the context of war.

When I called one of my best buddies back in San Diego, Eric Luna, and asked him if he knew how to get a dog out of Iraq, I heard nothing for a long time but some static. "Hey, Easy E, you still there?" I said.

"Yeah, man, I'm here. What did you just say?"

"Puppy. I have a puppy. Can you help me figure out how to get him out?"

Eric collected his wits. "Sure, man. Yeah, anything you want."

I returned to the main base with Lava on Thanksgiving Day in a Humvee—which, after serial bombardments, firefights and crashes, looked more like a secondhand stock car. Lava loved the loud trip; he perched on my lap and drooled. Once safely at Camp Fallujah, I spoke to the military dog handlers. The working dogs made up an elite unit that out-specialized any weaponry or high-tech mapping systems the U.S. armed forces possessed.

When I asked if Lava could hide out in one of their kennels, the handlers shook their heads. "Can't help you, sir." They said that the closest military vet who could give Lava vaccinations worked in Baghdad—some forty treacherous miles away. They doubted he'd be able to help. They wished me luck, though, and gave me what I suspected was some very expensive dog food.

When I contacted the military vet in Baghdad, he respectfully reiterated General Order 1-A, adding that diseases such as leishmaniasis, hydatid disease and rabies were common among stray dogs in Iraq. "My apparent lack of concern isn't due to not caring," he wrote. "I'm simply following orders."

Well, shoot. But I wasn't about to stop there. I'd already snuck Lava into the officers' building, where he slept with me on a cot. On the computer, I was Googling anything I could think of—puppy passport, help Marine help puppy. I felt frantic about Lava's fate. Yes, I was a Marine, brave to the point of insanity. But I'd be damned if I was going to let anyone shoot my puppy.

For most of January and February 2005, I worked at the Joint Task Force in Balad, replacing a lieutenant colonel there. I had great accommodations: a trailer with a real bed, a refrigerator, a wall locker. We also had a gym and plasma TVs in our command center. It might have been a great mission, except I worried about Lava. I knew he was safe with the Marines back at Camp Fallujah, but I was trying to save his life.

For a while Corporal Matt Hammond watched him, even building him a little plywood hooch, which the guys filled with toys and blankets and hid in the commanding general's personal security detachment, the last place on earth anyone would think to look. Then we came up with a plan to get Lava to Baghdad, where he would be vaccinated. The guys managed to convoy there, and at a prearranged time and place handed Lava off to journalist Anne Garrels, whom I'd become friendly with and who promised, by e-mail, to watch him for a few weeks at her National Public Radio (NPR) compound.

The hand-off was a bit of an ordeal, I heard later. Matt struggled to remain emotionless, while Anne grabbed Lava and left. Lava didn't have a collar or a leash, so she had to carry the now-large puppy back to the car. Luckily her Iraqi driver didn't object; most Iraqis did not like dogs. When I read Anne's e-mail from Baghdad, not even Patton's presence could have kept my tears from flowing. "Just to confirm that Lava is safely with me . . ."

Was I a gutless wimp? Maybe.

Anne would e-mail me with updates whenever she could: "Lava is happy." "He's incredibly affectionate." "He sits beautifully."

Meanwhile, a man she knew in Iraq, someone I'll call Sam to protect his identity, managed to locate a vet and get Lava all his shots and proper documentation. Before long, Anne had to leave Baghdad, while I was assigned to patrol the Syrian border until leaving for the States. By now, I had learned about Ken Licklider, who owned Vohne Liche Kennels in Indiana. He was a former U.S. Air Force police-dog handler who trained dogs for search-and-seizure work; many of his dogs were used by the military to sniff out bombs in Iraq. There was a chance that Lava could fly out with Ken's dogs and handlers to the United States. "It means putting Lava on a transport with them," John Van Zante told me.

John, of the Helen Woodward Animal Center in California,

and Kris Parlett, with the Iams dog food company, were my link to Ken. Iams had even offered to pay all the transport costs. Now we just had to sneak Lava out of the Red Zone in Baghdad, where he was hiding with journalists, to the military base in the Green Zone, the walled center of the city. John and Kris would take it from there. Me, by e-mail: "Thanks, John."

John: "We may actually put Lava on a plane. I hope this is it!"

Then, a worry. The kennel's overseas program coordinator: "Can you confirm that Lava has all his health and shot papers in order? Recently we ran into a problem with one of our dogs, and the military vet would not allow the dog to leave the country for an extra thirty days. I don't want that to happen to Lava." Neither did I. On top of that, I was leaving soon.

Sure enough, in early March I left Iraq, spent three days in a tent in Kuwait, and then flew to Shannon, Ireland. I was on my way home, but all I could think about as I drank pints with a bunch of other Marines was this: I just didn't see Lava making it to California to be with me. The plan to fly him out seemed too easy. You only get so much luck, my thinking went.

But as the weeks passed, the plan was cemented. In the Green Zone, David Mack (not his real name) reviewed Lava's documentation, including an international health certificate for live animals. Security around the Green Zone was cinched tighter than usual after reports of "irregularities" with the Iraqi elections. Demonstrations raged; mortars were launched.

At the NPR compound in the Red Zone, Lava was smuggled into a vehicle with a cameraman, since no animals were allowed to pass through. The vehicle drove to the first checkpoint. Sam waved goodbye. More mortar rounds were launched into the Green Zone. I sat at home in California and waited for an e-mail. And paced. And worried.

The vehicle sped through the dangerous streets, inching toward the checkpoint line. The driver stared forward. The cameraman counted rolls in the coiled barbed wire outside his window.

A bomb dog circled the vehicle as a guard reached through the window to check the cameraman's pass. The pass was good; it was the bomb dog's possible detection of Lava that was so threatening. But he was in search of only one thing, and when he didn't find it, he was off to the next vehicle. The guard scanned the pass and waved them into the Green Zone where, at that moment, the Iraqi government extended the country's emergency state by an additional thirty days. All of us waited. I paced some more.

Iraqi police patrolling the parade ground watched a vehicle trailing dust approach a location in the Green Zone and stop. They watched one man get out and shake hands with another, watched the two men exchange papers, watched a dog jump out of the car. They approached the vehicle and asked to see the papers. What was the dog's purpose?

"He's a working bomb dog," one of the men said. "I'm taking him back to my compound." They examined the papers, the dog, the man's face.

A motorcade then sped to Baghdad International Airport. One vehicle contained David, Lava in a crate, other people, and gunmen in bulletproof vests who guarded the doors and windows. The vehicles zoomed along on a highway where twelve people had been killed by bombs in the last month.

Finally, my dog arrived at the tarmac near a truck loaded with gear. "This is Lava," David told Brad Ridenour, a dog handler for Vohne Liche Kennels and another vital link in the chain. Soon after, I received a new e-mail.

I stared. I opened it and read. "As of 1600 hours," it said, "Lava is out of the country." For the second time in my adult life, I broke down and cried.

Brad flew with two other dog handlers to Amman, Jordan, where they passed through customs. They spent the night in a hotel in Amman, while the dogs were kept in an underground garage. As a result, Brad spent most of the night down there. Lava bounced around and wanted to play.

In the morning, the dog handlers were taken to Royal Jordanian, which would fly them to Chicago's O'Hare airport. Ken Licklider, meanwhile, drove to O'Hare, where he met up with John, Kris and others. They waited in the baggage area. Finally, Lava's crate came through.

John later explained, "That's when the dam just broke." He told me how he rushed Lava outside and exclaimed, "His first pee on American soil!"

And about Lava's behavior once they got to the hotel room, which John described as "Running around and around the room in circles. Wow."

And then John was finally calling me and saying, "He's here. He's safe. He's an American dog." John, Kris, and Lava flew into San Diego the next day.

Surrounded by the media, I waited at the Helen Woodward

Animal Center. Reporters asked me how I felt. Before I could answer, the airport van pulled up. I could see Lava through the window, see how big he'd gotten. I saw the same face, the same goofy look in his eyes, the tongue hanging out.

When Lava hopped down, stopped and stared at all the reporters, and then turned toward me, I looked a little above his head. That way I didn't see the recognition cross his face, didn't see past and future connect in his eyes. Because if I did, I knew I'd lose it then and there, and none of my comrades in the U.S. Marine Corps would ever speak to me again.

I'd wanted him to be alive. I wanted to know he was breathing and leaping after dust balls. If he was alive, then he would make it here to California and run on the beach and chase the mailman instead of strangers with guns. I'd wanted him to be alive almost more than anything I could think of.

Now Lava was headed my way. Fast. As fast as his legs could carry him. As I bent down to deflect the crash, that's when I saw the look in his eyes. It was an older version of the look he gave me when I first spotted him that day in Iraq: "I am going to kick your butt."

Film footage showed a dog barreling toward a well-composed Marine in uniform who bent down, caught the dog in mid-leap, stood up and turned circles with his face buried in the dog's fur. Lava was safe. He was home.

OUR COW NAMED
TIGER LILY

BY PENNY PORTER

For years on our Arizona ranch, we had raised purebred Here-fords, beautiful white-faced beef cattle. Knowing that one day they would be sent to market, my husband, Bill, always warned: "Don't ever get emotionally attached to a cow."

"Me?" I said, laughing. "Never! We've got six children to love and care for, and plenty of pets."

Then one Monday morning after chores, Bill came in, an odd grin on his face. "Wait till you see the stray calf that walked in last night."

By ranching custom, any stray that wanders onto your prop-erty is yours unless you know who owns it, or unless the owner appears.

I hurried to the barns. A vision flashed across my mind: a curly, fluffy adorable little calf, just like the rest of our Hereford babies.

I opened the gate, and there, leaning against the fence, its head hanging to the ground, stood the ugliest rail-bodied, bandy-legged heifer calf I'd ever seen. She was filthy, cut and bleeding. Her bowed ribs stuck out like jail bars, and her nose bristled with cactus quills, infection and flies.

"Let's get some penicillin and vitamins into her," Bill said. "Then we'll give her a bottle."

I removed the quills and plunged two medicine-filled hypodermic needles into her thigh. The poor little creature never flinched.

"Don't worry," Bill said. "I'll take her to auction Friday. But can you bottle-feed her till then?"

Soon the orphan was dashing to the gate when she heard me coming. She loved her bottle feeding—and, I guessed, I was now her mama.

Althought I hadn't forgotten Bill's warning, I realized that I'd fallen for this ugly crossbreed we didn't want or need. I couldn't let her be taken to auction.

"But she's useless to us," Bill said.

"Well, maybe someday Tiger Lily can replace Valentine as our nurse cow," I suggested.

"Tiger Lily?"

"Yes, well . . . the children dreamed up that name after looking at magazine photos of lilies. They thought the tiger lily was the prettiest."

"Tiger Lily?" Bill said again. "Whoever heard of a cow named Tiger Lily?"

"Nobody till now." I smiled.

"Well, she's your responsibility," he said, and I could almost hear the unspoken words *I don't have time to be fixing baby bottles.*

Almost from the start, Tiger Lily was trouble. She jumped

into watering troughs, broke valves and flooded the barns and corrals in the night. She got stuck under a fence and had to be dug out. One day, being overly inquisitive, she was even bitten on the nose by a rattlesnake. Her face ballooned, and I spent the night holding ice packs in place and praying the antidote would save her.

When tiny horns appeared on Tiger Lily's head, an itchy spot at their base drove her nearly crazy. Scratching the itch on the corral fence brought little relief. The gate latch was far more effective, and she found that, with a slight twist of her head and horns, the gate would open. Before long, unlatching the gate and searching for her "mama" became Tiger Lily's goal.

One hot morning, I was stunned when the handle on our kitchen screen door rattled and Tiger Lily, now over 300 pounds, pushed her way in. Snorting, she poked her nose in the breadbox, and scanned the breakfast table with her enormous brown eyes. Then she tried scratching her horns against the table, lifting it right off the floor.

"She'll have to go out to pasture with the yearling heifers," Bill ordered, "and live like a normal cow—behind barbed wire."

So at 9 months, Tiger Lily joined our other cattle—even though Bill considered her the weed among the flowers of his herd.

Certainly she stood out, with her huge, gangly brown body, and long, bony back and hips I could hang my jacket on. I went out to see her often and always found her grazing peacefully. She never forgot me. All I had to do was call, "Tiger Lily! Hi, girl. Remember me?" and she would moo and amble over to have the itchy place scratched.

But it wasn't unusual to find her in the mornings with her horns stuck in a barbed-wire gate. "What a KLUTZ!" Bill would groan as he struggled to get her loose.

When she was 3 years old Tiger Lily got into the biggest and most serious trouble of all. We faced a difficult calving season. Some of the babies were "too big." Seven calves had died during the birthing process, a danger when breeding young heifers to a new bull. But with a "night patrol," Bill, my 18-year-old son Scott and I had saved twenty-one calves by getting to the heifer in time, roping her, and pulling the oversized baby out before it suffocated in the birth canal.

One February night it was well below freezing at 1 a.m. as I headed for the calving pasture on my three-wheel all-terrain vehicle. I cruised slowly among the pregnant Herefords. Tiger Lily, pregnant for the first time, was not among them. Cows about to give birth often seek a distant corner of the pasture.

My hands and feet were numb when I finally found her, trapped in an old concrete irrigation ditch. She had rolled into the tapered, vise-like tomb while struggling to deliver her "too big" calf. There was blood everywhere, and the tips of her horns had snapped off in her frantic effort to escape. The still form of her newborn lay a few feet farther along the ditch—dead.

The pitiful sight was more than I wanted to deal with at that troubling moment. So, straining, I dragged the poor little thing farther away. Then I ran back and sank to my knees beside Tiger Lily.

"Oh, Tiger," my voice broke, "why did this have to happen to you?"

Terror rimmed her soft brown eyes, and when I placed my hand on her velvet nose, a strangled moan rose from her half-ton body. She undoubtedly smelled her calf on my hands.

She was barely breathing. Pressure from the sloping sides of the ditch was crushing her lungs. God help her, I prayed as I ran home to wake Bill.

"Honey! Tiger Lily's dying!" I said. "We're going to need the tractor with the front-end loader. Hurry!"

I ran to the barn for chains, ropes, and an oxygen tank, and threw everything into our truck. Scott jumped in beside me.

When we finally reached Tiger Lily, her eyes were closed. "I think she's dead," I whispered.

Scott clamped the huge oxygen mask over her nose and mouth, and when Bill pulled up with the tractor, they wrapped ropes and chains around Tiger Lily, attached them to the hydraulic boom and pulled her out of the ditch. Then scooping her up carefully in the front-end loader, they drove her home.

The vet arrived at dawn. "Her calf was so large it broke her pelvis and caused nerve damage," he said after examining her. "I'm afraid she's paralyzed." Tiger Lily lay on the ground where Bill had placed her.

"Will she walk again, Doc?" Bill asked.

"There's always hope—if she lives."

For days Tiger Lily neither ate nor drank. We took turns massaging her back legs but there was no sign of movement. I attempted to stroke that spot at the base of her horns, but she tossed her head. She wanted no part of me. She associated me with her recent trauma, and perhaps even the loss of her calf.

Three days later, Scott came in from the calving pasture with a rejected newborn. It had absolutely no hair. Its skin was crimson. It weighed perhaps 30 pounds. The average among our newborns was 75. As Scott stood the poor little thing on the ground, it trembled and bawled long and piteously.

Then, an extraordinary and wonderful thing happened. Mooing softly, Tiger Lily answered. Something was stirring deep inside her. Something only mothers know. She mooed again, and the hairless calf tottered toward her. When their moist noses touched, Tiger Lily began licking the tiny face. Soon he was nuzzling her sunken belly, searching until finally he found her warm milk.

By nightfall, Tiger Lily had drunk water by herself and eaten some hay for the first time. When I checked her before going to bed that night, she was contentedly chewing her cud.

We named the calf the "Hairless Wonder," which the children soon shortened to "Hairy," then "Harry." As Harry grew stronger, we could see he wanted Tiger Lily to get up. He charged into her, kicked her, butted her in the rump. After three weeks, we decided it was time to give an assist.

Bill and Scott made a canvas sling and rolled Tiger Lily onto it. Once again, the front-end loader was used to lift her. When she was upright with her hoofs planted on the ground, Harry raced around, wild with anticipation.

For six weeks Tiger Lily hung by day, and was lowered to rest at night. May arrived, the sling was removed, and a healed Tiger Lily stood unaided. But she wouldn't walk. Bill and Scott placed her food and water just out of reach, but the next morning she was still riveted to the same spot.

"I have an idea," Bill said to me one day. "Since she really seems to have it in for you, we'll chase Harry, and you make a grab for him. Maybe she'll take a step trying to protect him." *Would she think I would take Harry away, the way she seemed to think I'd taken her first baby?*

Bill and Scott gave chase. Sure enough, Tiger Lily began snorting and pawing with a front hoof. Then I managed to grab Harry. He bellowed loudly. Tiger Lily headed straight toward me, and suddenly I was on the ground, my mouth full of dirt. Scott and Bill tried not to laugh as they helped me up.

For the next seven months, Tiger Lily, with Harry at her side, lived an idyllic life as her calf grew a fine fur coat, and soon reached 600 pounds. "Tiger Lily's going to make a fine nurse cow," said Bill. Then the day came for Harry to be weaned.

The loss of the calf that had given her a second chance at life devastated Tiger Lily. She lost 100 pounds. This poor, downtrodden weed among all the flowers of our herd spent her days calling Harry. I wanted to comfort her, but I still couldn't get near. Once again her calf had been taken from her, and she wanted nothing to do with me.

A year went by, and Tiger Lily gave birth to twin heifers. They thrived on her rich, abundant milk, as did a third calf who came to "rob" a little that year because his own mother didn't have enough.

At long last Tiger Lily seemed content. She was needed, and a pattern was set for the next fifteen years. During this time, she raised 16 calves of her own, countless foster offspring and a never-ending parade of hungry "robbers" who wanted just a little bit more.

Tiger Lily was 19 when arthritis in her back legs finally became so severe that we knew we would soon have to put her down. It seemed that my Tiger Lily, almost 20 years old now, sensed the last summer had come. One day, she walked slowly across the field, stretched her head over the fence and mooed softly.

It was the moment I'd been waiting for. She had been *my* cow, and I believed that despite the pain and hurt she still loved me.

Her back swayed like a well-used hammock, she could barely walk, and her bony hips stuck out like antique airplane wings. I moved closer.

"Hi, old girl. Remember me?"

She looked up with those soft brown eyes and then very slowly lowered her head. I recognized the signal from all those years before. She wanted me to scratch the spot that itched at the base of her horns. I knew then, at last, that I was forgiven. Once again, we were together.

Except that something had changed: Over the years, the stray that had wandered into our hearts, a weed among her kind, had become the favorite flower in our fields.

FOR THE LOVE OF STRANGERS

THE ANGEL FOR LOST CHILDREN

BY BARBARA SANDE DIMMITT

Richard Paul Evans was physically and emotionally spent. It was November 1992, and the Salt Lake City advertising executive had come off a breakneck few months of eighteen-hour days. His home life had suffered. The devoted husband and father ached for time lost with his daughters, six-year-old Jenna and four-year-old Allyson. With Christmas near, he wanted to convey how precious his girls were to him. They loved it when he read to them, so a book written by him from the heart seemed the perfect gift.

Evans began to sketch out the story of a father who pours all his energies into his job, selfishly sacrificing his family along the way. But troubling scenes of a mother mourning the death of a child kept intruding on Evans's thoughts.

What did this have to do with his story? he wondered. One night the answer came from a childhood memory.

When Rick Evans was 4, he'd found his mother, June, quietly weeping one afternoon in her bedroom. He asked her why.

"This would have been Sue's birthday," she said softly. Two years before, the boy knew, his mother had delivered a stillborn daughter. With a child's bewildered empathy, Rick reached out and gave her a hug.

The topic of Sue rarely came up in family conversation after that. Rick's father, with a large family to support, stoically threw himself into running his construction business. If the loss of his daughter weighed on his mind, he never gave the merest hint. But there were times when Rick could tell his mother still mourned.

Now, more than twenty-five years later, the sister he'd never known seemed mystically real. And he understood how this puzzle piece would fit into his book. The story would deal with the twin tragedies of parenthood: the abrupt loss of a child through death and the slower loss of a child through neglect.

The subject seemed dark, depressing. But Evans, inspired, worked to shape a message of love to his girls and one of healing to his mother.

As the book neared completion, he struggled for an image stark enough to portray a parent's despair at losing a child. He recalled an elderly neighbor's reminiscence about playing in the city cemetery as a child, and seeing a woman come each day to weep beneath a statue of an angel marking a child's grave.

The poignant devotion of the mother and the tender symbolism of the angel struck Evans. After changing some of the elements, he added similar imagery to his book. The slim volume exceeded Evans's hopes at the family's traditional Christmas Eve celebration. He opened a copy and showed it to his mother, pointing to the dedication: "To Sue." "Mom, I think she gave me the story for you," he said. June Evans took her son into her arms and thanked him in an emotion-choked whisper, as Evans's father, David, stood quietly nearby.

Later, with Jenna and Allyson sitting spellbound, Evans read them the story.

Then, pleased at its reception, he put the book on a shelf where it would be handy the next time his daughters wanted to hear it.

The Christmas Box, though, seemed bent on pursuing a different destiny. Bound photocopies Evans gave family members were passed along from friend to friend.

Strangers called to tell him how much the book meant to them. Soon local bookstores were calling Evans and asking him for copies.

Urged by readers, Evans sent *The Christmas Box* to local publishers, who quickly rejected it. Evans and his wife, Keri, then risked their own savings to self-publish eight thousand copies in August 1993. They had no idea the book's word-of-mouth reputation would rocket it to best-seller lists and draw offers from major New York publishers.

By November local book sales were accelerating, and Evans was regularly attending book signings. At one event, a sad-eyed woman approached him.

"Would you like me to autograph a book?" he asked.

She shook her head. "I've read it, but you're not old enough to be the man in the book," she said. "The story isn't true."

"No," he replied. "It's fiction."

"I wanted to lay a flower at the angel," she murmured. Then she drifted away.

Evans was dumbstruck. He recognized the suffering in her face; at virtually every book signing he'd seen the same look on people who talked to him about children they'd lost. They always mentioned how healing *The Christmas Box* was for them. Most found the scene involving the stone angel especially cathartic and comforting. Never had Evans imagined that the absence of a real statue might cause pain.

Troubled, Evans then described his encounter to the book's distributor. "We get lots of calls wanting to know where the angel is," one of the distributor's salesmen said to him.

Now Evans himself wanted to know. He asked his elderly neighbor to show him, but they found only low-lying headstones in the part of the cemetery she remembered. Any statue that might have been there seventy years before was long gone.

To Evans, the angel had been a compelling literary device. Perhaps too compelling. As the book's following grew, people from across the country traveled to Salt Lake City, searching for comfort they'd never find. Evans came to think there was only one thing for him to do: Erect a new stone angel for those mourners to visit, and find healing.

Upon hearing his plan, June Evans was deeply moved. "I've never had a place to go to mourn. Sue was never buried; that's the way things were done. I think other people thought it would be easier for your father and me if we just tried to forget."

Evans couldn't fathom how he'd deal with such a loss himself. But he understood that, thirty years before, David Evans would have been more a spectator than a participant in the birthing process. And he'd had to be strong in the face of his daughter's death.

In debt to his parents, David, the father of seven, had been working on a degree in social work, hoping it would lead to steadier income than he'd found in construction. He probably was so concerned about his wife's health and the needs of the family that he willed away any grief about the child.

Yet June was still hurting. Clearly, silence and isolation could preserve, even heighten, the feeling of loss.

Certain that his mother and countless others needed this healing place, Evans focused on finding a suitable angel. In September 1994 he met with Ortho Fairbanks, a well-known sculptor, and his wife, Myrna. It turned out the Fairbanks family had a special reason to want to get involved; they, too, had lost a child.

The author described his vision of a statue of a child with angel's wings and the dedication he planned to hold in early December. Fairbanks told Evans that a stone statue could take years. A bronze statue with a stonelike patina was the best bet, but even that would usually take six months to a year. However, deeply moved by Evans's mission, Fairbanks promised he'd somehow finish the angel on schedule.

The sculptor kept his word. He enlisted the aid of his son, also a sculptor, and the two worked around the clock. Meanwhile Evans and the cemetery sexton identified land where the statue might be erected. Two days before the deadline, the Christmas Box Angel was ready to be lowered into place overlooking Salt Lake City.

On the evening of December 6, 1994, more than four hundred people trudged through rain-slicked snow to the upper slope of the cemetery. Tiny candles, protected by umbrellas and cupped by palms, flickered in the darkness. Local dignitaries spoke, but few in the audience took their eyes from the angel.

She stood slightly larger than life-size atop a granite base. Two spotlights illuminated her outstretched arms from below, casting a glow on her upturned face. Those who looked closely could see the word Hope blended into the feathered texture of her right wing.

"Bright angels around my darling shall stand," sang a choir of children, their sweet, unschooled voices carrying over the hillside. "They will guard thee from harms, thou shalt wake in my arms." Then came the moment Evans had anticipated for months. His petite mother, holding a rose whiter than her own hair, approached the angel. She knelt and gently laid the flower at the angel's base. Looking on, Evans found himself blinking away tears. He watched as she stood and turned, her eyes shining in a face smoothed by relief. Evans took his mother in his arms. "Finally," she said, "we have a place for Sue."

People now filed past the angel until white flowers cascaded over the base of the statue like a long-trained skirt. Someone placed a rose across the angel's outstretched palms, and soon the statue's arms were filled. Parents left tiny toys, pictures and other mementos of their children.

Evans stood in the drizzle and watched the angel at work. He had asked Ortho Fairbanks to sculpt an angel with arms raised as if asking to be lifted. But judging by the peaceful expressions on the candlelit faces around him, this angel was reaching out more to comfort than to be comforted. "Come and lay your burdens here," she seemed to be saying. And one by one, her visitors did.

Evans surveyed the crowd, and his eyes once more went to his mother. He'd completed his gift to her and felt as if nothing could surpass this moment. But then he glanced beside her and noticed his father.

Tears were streaming down David Evans's cheeks. In the look of astonished anguish on the older man's face, the son read a tale of suffering long held at bay. Surrounded by strangers drawn close by their common tragedy, Evans's parents turned to each other and embraced. Above them hovered the angel, glistening in the night rain.

THIS BOY'S LIFE

BY NEAL HIRSCHFELD

One day last March, John Barrows and his wife, Cheryl, reached for each other's hand, took a deep breath, and pushed through the doors into a hotel meeting room in Raleigh, North Carolina. With them were their three sons, Danny, Shaun, and Chris, all strapping six-footers. The only one missing was their youngest boy, Timothy.

Entering the room, John and Cheryl were immediately surrounded by two dozen strangers, some of whom had traveled nearly a thousand miles just to meet the Barrows family. At first, they all stood about awkwardly, their conversation stilted. Then 69-year-old Huey Lumley of Cameron, North Carolina, stepped forward and introduced himself. A retired phosphate-mining supervisor, Lumley had long suffered from congestive heart failure. Two and a half years ago, after enduring multiple heart attacks and triple bypass surgery, he was desperately ill. One doctor told Lumley that he probably would not live out the year, and suggested his family start making funeral arrangements. Yet here he was in Raleigh, fit and chipper, free at last of the chronic chest pains and labored breathing, boasting about riding his exercise bicycle ten miles a day.

As John Barrows greeted him, Lumley said softly, "I am so thankful that there are people like you and your family." Barrows leaned forward and wrapped Lumley in a bearhug. "God bless you," he whispered. At that moment, as he stood torso to torso with Huey Lumley, feeling the life-sustaining thump, thump, thump that pulsated through Lumley's chest, John Barrows was actually feeling the beat of his 15-year-old son Tim's heart.

It was the summer of 1998 when Barrows, an executive for IBM, and his wife first learned that Tim had decided to become an organ donor. Bursting excitedly into their Raleigh home one afternoon, Tim waved the learner's permit he had just received, then handed the precious card to his dad. John studied the photo of his son, looking like a young James Dean, cool smirk and all. It was only when he moved his thumb that he spotted the small red heart in the lower- right-hand corner. He knew immediately what it meant.

A former U.S. Army lieutenant and a highly decorated veteran of combat in Vietnam, John also knew what a human body could look like after violent death or traumatic injury. For a long moment his gaze was riveted to the heart. Then he locked eyes with his boy. "Have you given this a lot of thought? Is it what you really want to do?"

Tim dropped his playful exuberance. Two months earlier he

had been a passenger in a sport utility vehicle that was hit by another car. The collision had sent him to the hospital with glass shards in his eyes, nose, throat, and ears. So he knew just how fragile life could be.

"Yes, Dad, it's something that I really want to do." John Barrows hugged his son.

"I love you," he told Tim.

Both John and Cheryl were deeply moved by the boy's courage and generosity of spirit. At the time, they chose not to dwell on the possibility that, some day, his pledge might need to be honored.

Then, barely three months later, the unthinkable happened. On Halloween night 1998, as Tim rode in a Chevy Blazer driven by his 16-year-old friend Scott Miller, their vehicle was broadsided by a van speeding along at more than 70 m.p.h. The van's driver, 25-year-old Oscar Melendez, had plopped himself behind the wheel with nearly twice the legal limit of alcohol in his blood. Both boys suffered severe injuries to their brains. Melendez, who had convictions for drunk driving, assault, and fraud, suffered a hip injury.

Summoned to WakeMed hospital late that night, John and Cheryl Barrows were given the grim news: Their son Tim was not expected to survive more than fifteen hours. His friend, too, was dying. The grief was unbearable. As both boys slipped away, words seemed futile; all John and Cheryl could do was hold each other tight. Numbly, they stood by while an elderly Catholic priest gave Tim the last rites. Finally, gathering their other three sons and their nephew, Scott Pettingill, outside the

ICU, John and Cheryl reminded them of Tim's desire to become an organ donor. They talked together, asked questions, tried to grasp what it now meant. But there was never any real doubt: They would honor Tim's wish.

When the Barrows family walked into that Raleigh meeting room early last spring, Huey Lumley was not the only organ recipient on hand. Thanks to Carolina Donor Services, a local organ-procurement organization, many others had been located and invited.

Bobby Wester, 43, a tall, goateed house-construction worker from Rocky Mount, North Carolina, told of his desperate, two-and-a-half-year wait for a liver transplant. Infected with hepatitis C, yellow with jaundice and taking more than twenty different pills a day, Wester was so sick that he could barely get out of bed. The cause of his illness, doctors believed, was infection from a small tattoo that had been etched into his left arm twenty-five years earlier—a dare from his Army buddies. When one of his blood vessels burst and he began spitting up blood, Wester figured his days were numbered. Then, during a six-hour operation at the Duke University Medical Center in November 1998, Wester was given Tim's liver. Now, more than two years later, Wester was going at full throttle, even playing league softball and golf. "Heck, we're going fishing for bass later today," he told some of the others in the room, gesturing over to his teenage daughter.

Nearby, 5-year-old Joshua Knight, who had arrived from Little Rock, Arkansas, with his mom, Carole, and his dad, Brian, was playing a game of hide-and-seek with his 3-year-old twin siblings. Joshua was born with Denys-Drash syndrome, a rare genetic disease that caused his kidneys to lose protein and damaged his immune system. At the age of 11 months, both his kidneys were surgically removed and Joshua was forced to go on dialysis.

Over the next two years he lay hooked up to machines twelve hours each night, while being subjected to frequent and painful injections. Even on dialysis, Joshua tired easily and was unable to walk more than three blocks at a time. His skin turned a yellowish color and his breath had a pungent odor. As a nurse, Joshua's mom knew firsthand what it was like to watch a child on dialysis die of complications. Then in 1998, during an operation at the Arkansas Children's Hospital, Joshua Knight received one of Tim's kidneys. And, for all intents and purposes, he was born again.

The night after the operation, Joshua leapt up in his hospital bed and tried to fly into one of the cartoons playing on the television set. Two weeks later his color turned rosy pink; he was brimming with so much energy that he began to run in place furiously, like a plane revving its engines for takeoff. And for the last couple of years he'd been no less spirited, racing around the yard on his tricycle and roughhousing with his little brother and sister. Clad in his Buzz Lightyear T-shirt, Joshua scooted about the Raleigh meeting room, proudly jiggling his two loose front teeth for all to see. For weeks he had been telling his parents how much he wanted to meet his donor family (although his sister Emma remained convinced they were there to meet his "donut family").

Not all of the organ recipients were able to come to Raleigh. Virgal Neace, a 65-year-old former welding supervisor in Lombard, Illinois, who had received one of Tim's kidneys, was crestfallen that he hadn't learned about the gathering in time to make the travel arrangements. In a phone conversation two days earlier, Neace spoke of battling coronary and circulatory problems so severe that they necessitated open-heart surgery and seventy blood transfusions. Growing steadily weaker, he was forced to stop working on Good Friday, 1990.

"By the time I got Tim's kidney," he told John Barrows, "I couldn't even pull the starter on my lawn mower. The pain was just so bad." But now Neace was cutting his own grass again, blowing the snow—doing so many things that make him feel alive and useful. "I just can't tell you what it's like to have my strength return, to feel like I'm thirty-five again."

Also missing was Katherine Mary Felicio, a woman from Sanford, North Carolina, who had received one of Tim's lungs. A lifelong smoker afflicted with chronic emphysema, Felicio had lived for a year and a half after her transplant. She died in April 2000 at age 59. But her family, grateful for the extra time her new lung had given her, had come to Raleigh to say thank you, nonetheless. "Mom would have wanted us to be here," her son Robert, Jr., told John and Cheryl.

After the introductions were completed, John and Cheryl asked all the organ recipients and their families to take seats. The room fell quiet as the two began to speak. John Barrows talked first about their emotional courtroom confrontation. in July 1999 with Oscar Melendez, the driver who had killed Tim and his friend. Melendez pleaded guilty to two counts of second-degree murder, expecting leniency from the court in return. Instead, the judge sentenced him to thirty-one and a half to thrity-nine years in prison.

They talked about the seventy-six thousand other people across the country who were still on waiting lists for organ transplants. And how, because of the acute shortage of donors, only a third of those desperately ill patients might ever realize their dream—while another third would die waiting.

But mostly John and Cheryl talked about Tim. The youngest and smallest of their four boys, Tim had been a rebel. A jokester. A kid who never bragged or boasted, and seemed to have a million best friends. "Before today, I so wished that all of you could have known Tim," John Barrows told everyone. "Now you do."

"My son's death was a tragedy," Cheryl said. "But the fact that he was able to help so many people makes us proud. We want you to go away from here today being happy. Our son would have wanted you to be happy too."

While John and Cheryl spoke, Tim's learner's permit was passed around the table. On the face of the card, everyone could see Tim's impish, smiling countenance. And, of course, the small red heart that had so profoundly altered all their lives. As the card moved from person to person, the room grew somber and still. Bobby Wester reached for a handkerchief and buried his face in his hands. When the card reached Tim's brother Shaun, he began to weep. Suddenly Wester rose from his seat, circled the table and dropped to his knees by Shaun's side. Then he wrapped his arms around the boy's shoulders and sobbed right along with him.

In the end, Tim Barrows's "gift of life" proved to be a remarkably generous one. Besides the donation of most of his major organs—his heart, one lung, liver and both kidneys—Tim's corneas were given to a 42-year-old man in New Jersey and a 24-year-old woman in Raleigh. A total of three hundred and nineteen tissue grafts from his body were distributed nationwide, with at least one hundred patients already having been recipients. Bone and tissue from these grafts were utilized in operations on nineteen orthopedic patients in six different states, and were prepared for dental surgeries in at least a dozen more states. Behind these remarkable numbers were scores of individual lives, changed forever. And none were more dramatically helped than those who gathered in Raleigh to honor Tim's lifesaving bequest.

It was Joshua Knight's dad, Brian, who summed it up best: "There just aren't any words in the English language to express what we feel. The words thank you aren't enough. It's something bigger than thank you . . . way bigger. And every one of us feels it."

CROSSING THE LINE:
A CIVIL WAR LOVE STORY

BY CHRIS BOHJALIAN

February winds coil across the thick ice of Lake Memphrema-
gog to the small Vermont town of Newport. Ice-fishing shan-
ties dot the surface of the lake like houses on a Monopoly
board. The hamlet itself sits on a series of hills that slope into
the water from three sides, with a cemetery just beyond the
easternmost one. The snow this morning is thick. It covers
the headstones and climbs partway up the rectangular granite
spire that rises a dozen feet into the air and marks the remains
of the Civil War soldier Henry Edson Bedell.

Bedell was a Union lieutenant from the nearby village of
Westfield. He fought with the Vermont Brigade from 1862 until Confederate cannon fire ripped apart his leg and mangled
his hand in September 1864. Bedell, a footnote in Civil War
history, is considered a hero in these parts. His story is one
that intrigues historians and romantics alike, for it is tied to a
woman, Bettie Van Metre, whose grave lies six hundred and
forty miles to the south in Virginia's lush Shenandoah Valley.

Van Metre was a young Southern bride with two brothers in the Confederate army and a soldier husband lost in the vast labyrinth of Yankee prison camps. Then she was brought face to face with the enemy in the bloodied and broken body of Henry Bedell. Their small, personal story is buried in the midst of the epic conflagration that surrounded them. It's there in the letters that remain in library archives, in the sweeping script of diary entries written at dusk, in fading silver print photographs. In graveyards in Virginia and Vermont, in two accounts by their contemporaries (one by Bedell's commanding officer, Aldace Walker) and in family legend handed down over the years. These artifacts and voices combine to offer a saga of daring, risk, betrayal and, perhaps, something more—something like a love story.

It rained throughout the second week of September in the Shenandoah Valley in 1864, and the Vermont Brigade dug rifle pits in the muddy clay and slept in soggy tents. Hardtack turned sodden, sugar melted, salt dissolved. Henry Bedell had served often on picket duty, and by the middle of the month his wool uniform was constantly damp. Bedell was a good soldier. He enlisted as a corporal in the summer of 1862, was promoted to sergeant, and then to second lieutenant in January 1864.

Born in Westfield in 1836, Bedell was a big man for the mid-19th century, towering above most at six feet, two inches. And he was as handsome as he was rugged. He was a farmer with a hundred hardscrabble Vermont acres, married to a schoolteacher named Emeline. It took a firm commitment for Bedell to enlist in the Union army. It would mean leaving not only Emeline, but their three children and an adopted nephew as well.

After spending his first months in the army guarding Washington, D.C., suddenly in the spring and summer of 1864, Bedell's brigade was thrust into some of the very worst fighting of the war: the battles of Spotsylvania, Cold Harbor and Petersburg. At Spotsylvania, two weeks of arduous hand-to-hand carnage in the woods left eighteen thousand Union casualties. Bedell was wounded in the neck, and days after he returned to the skirmish lines, his friend Lieutenant Sherman was shot through the head as he stood beside him.

On September 13, Bedell was near Berryville, where his brigade encountered Confederate troops. A Union artillery battery opened fire to assess the exact location of the enemy, led by Gen. Jubal Early. Bedell heard the cannon fire as the shells whizzed toward the far side of Opequon Creek, and felt a surge of adrenaline: His army was upping the ante in this little clash. Early was a pit bull and he responded in kind. He moved an even larger battery to a hill on his side of the stream, hoping to silence the Northern guns. A young Middlebury College valedictorian named Aldace Walker, a captain, saw the Rebel artillery, but couldn't get near his own battery to warn them. Walker's horse was terrified by the sound of the explosions and the smell of the gunpowder. And so instead he rode toward the trees to warn the men. Bedell was there, waiting, as the cannons started bringing down the thunder.

In September 1864, with her husband in a Union prison

camp, 24-year-old Bettie Van Metre was living on a once-fertile valley farm. The Shenandoah River ran through it, driving the wooden wheels and gears of a mill that provided the family income. With her was her 10-year-old niece and two of her husband's former slaves, a husband and wife named Dick and Ginny Runner.

Bettie was born Elizabeth Keyser. She grew up in the Luray Valley, in the southern part of the Shenandoah, in a village called Honeyville. We do not know how she met her husband, James Van Metre, a curiosity if only because James lived in Berryville, over sixty miles to the north—a considerable distance in those times. But he married the blue-eyed girl in the late 1850s. And she moved to the one-hundred-acre farm where he had built the gristmill that contained their living quarters.

With James at war now for nearly two years, Bettie was barely scraping by. Moreover, that summer Ulysses Grant had visited Phil Sheridan, the intense, gritty commander of the Union Army of the Shenandoah. Grant's instructions to his men: Destroy the fertile valley so thoroughly that "crows flying over it will have to carry their provender with them." Sheridan did just that—and some of his troops carried out the order with particular zeal. That autumn, they were confiscating the livestock, burning fields and barns, and reducing the breadbasket of the Confederate army to ash. This meant that not only would Bettie and her niece have little to eat on their own farm, but their neighbors no longer had grain to bring to the Van Metre mill. Their already meager wartime diet would have fallen to near starvation standards.

Hidden with his men in a thicket of wood, Bedell felt the Confederate cannon balls splinter the trees around him and shake the ground. Smoke and the scent of shattered pine filled the forest. The first shells from the Rebel battery landed smack in the mass of huddled Yankees. Suddenly a shell burst into him, ripping open his left leg and his right hand. The blast sent Bedell sprawling, and reflexively he reached down for his knee. Though three fingers on his hand were hanging by threads, he understood the leg wound was by far the more serious: The bones were pulverized above his knee, the muscles and flesh had been mangled into a pulpy stew, and his femoral artery was pumping blood into the rich soil of the Shenandoah Valley like a garden hose. Despite his wounds, he was fully conscious.

"Cord it! Cord it!" he bellowed when he saw Walker, his captain and friend, dismounting. "Don't let me bleed to death!"

Walker took a rope and succeeded in wrapping a tourniquet around what was left of Bedell's thigh, using a rifle's ramrod to twist the twine tight. Unfortunately, he turned the bar one time too many, the rope broke, and once more Bedell's blood was turning the dirt beneath his leg into swamp. Somewhere Walker found a second length of the rope, and this time, as Bedell was slipping into shock—he was shivering, despite the Shenandoah heat and fiery smog of battle—the tourniquet held. The desperate hemorrhaging slowed and Bedell grew quiet. Ironically, so did the Rebel shelling. This was one of a series of fights the North would win. And though Bedell may have guessed he was out of immediate danger, he must have known also that the tourniquet was going to cost him his leg.

The limb was amputated that afternoon. Such grisly work

took place in nearby farmhouses or hastily built field hospital tents, the surgeons and their assistants frequently naked from the waist up because it was easier to scrub the spattered blood off their skin than their clothes. They tended to work quickly, only occasionally rinsing off their bone saws. Bedell may have been dosed with chloroform or ether beforehand, or he may have settled for a swallow of whiskey. After cutting off the leg, Bedell's surgeons decided that if the patient survived the next day, they would do something about his hand. In the meantime, he was moved to a nearby house to rest. "The chances," Walker wrote home on the 14th, "are against his living."

But on the 15th Bedell was still alive, and so the surgeons decided to amputate the middle finger on his right hand and reset the broken bones in his other fingers. Bedell's story might easily have ended here. He might have continued to convalesce and been sent home with crutches later that autumn, or died of typhoid, malaria, or pneumonia in any one of the desperately overcrowded Union hospitals.

On the 16th, however, Grant told Sheridan that he wanted him to proceed more aggressively into the Shenandoah. With the army now geared to move south, all the wounded—including Bedell—were to be transported twenty miles north to Harpers Ferry. Bedell never made it. He lasted less than a mile in a horse-drawn ambulance, a covered but springless buckboard, before the jostling caused him to pass out from pain. He was returned to the second floor of the house where he had lain after surgery, with a pair of soldiers to protect him. Living on the first floor of the building were squatters, a married couple named Asbury. Though they were Southern sympathizers, the army paid them to prepare food for Bedell, and to give him whatever medicine he would need.

On the 19th, Sheridan's army continued south, leaving this corner of the Shenandoah open to Rebel forces. Bedell was being abandoned to his fate. His guards left almost immediately, either because they were frightened or because Bedell encouraged them to depart. Certainly they had good reason to be scared: Southerners in the Shenandoah that autumn had a particular hatred for the Yankee army. Sheridan was scorching the earth, and after the September battle of Winchester, Confederate raider John Mosby and a dashing young Union cavalry officer named George Custer began a brief but desperate game of reprisal one-upmanship. Custer's forces were executing partisans, and Mosby was delivering captured Union soldiers the same fate.

One of Bedell's guards told his superiors when he arrived in Harpers Ferry that the lieutenant was dead. In any case, a week after he was wounded, Bedell was alone on the second floor of a house in northern Virginia, one of the army's waterproof rubber blankets the sheet beneath his back. He was in constant, excruciating pain from the amputations, the broken bones and the grisly infections that were beginning to beset his leg and hand. He was too sick to be hungry, but he was thirsty in that stuffy room in September, and—since he couldn't rise from the floor—he was lying in trousers wet with his own urine and excrement. He was over six hundred miles from his wife, his children and his home. And the Asburys, he realized, had left him to die.

Dick Runner informed Bettie that there was a mortally wounded Union soldier in the house a half-mile up the road. He suggested that they bring the man food, and—hesitantly— she agreed to check in on him. When Bettie arrived at the home, Mrs. Asbury tried to stop her from venturing upstairs. "What would people say?" she asked, the threat in this case not being mere social estrangement but retribution from Confederate raiders. Bettie would not be bullied. Curious, she climbed the steps. As she entered the room, the awful stench from Bedell's wounds was enough to make her recoil. She watched him pull a corner of the blanket beneath him over his face with his left hand, and then she walked to the window for air. She was frightened by this large, faceless man on the floor, and decided finally that she'd leave. There was nothing she could do for him. This was no place for her.

But then the blanket slid off Bedell's face and she saw he was . . . sobbing. Not tearing, not crying. Sobbing. A man who towered over six feet was now sobbing shamelessly on the floor. She approached him, put the palm of her hand on his fevered forehead. She told him he needn't cry, but only because she wasn't sure what else she could say. "You remind me of my wife," he murmured, and she wondered if he was telling her this to excuse his sobs, or so she would trust him, or because—pure and simple—it was the truth. "Your dress . . . even your dress. It looks like the one she wore when I left her."

She nodded, her fingers damp with his sweat. "Would you write a letter to my wife?" he asked softly, and for a moment she pondered this request. Clearly he assumed he was going to die—and, in all likelihood, he was correct. She had seen an awful lot of death in this war, both here in the Shenandoah Valley and at Gettysburg, where she had gone to nurse her gravely wounded brother. The truth was, she decided, a dying Yankee looked exactly like a dying Rebel. Did the color of his uniform really matter? It shouldn't. Moreover, her husband was somewhere to the north: If James had been this badly injured—if he were dying—she would want a Yankee woman to take pity on him.

"A doctor first," she told him finally. "Then a letter."

Her family physician, a man named Osborne, put aside his Confederate sympathies and came to the house. With Bettie's help, the doctor cleaned the festering wounds and sponged the lieutenant's filthy body. They made him as comfortable as they could, perhaps on a bed of straw, and then Bettie asked Ginny Runner to stay and nurse him through the night. As Bettie left for home, she would have passed by Mrs. Asbury on her way out. The churlish, pitiless woman now knew that Bettie was providing comfort to the enemy.

Dr. Osborne told Bettie that Bedell was going to die without such 19th-century medical staples as quinine and whiskey. It was just that simple. And, he added, no Confederate physician in their corner of Virginia had such supplies these days. Osborne must have expected her to accept this grim news with the stoicism that marked so much of their lives in 1864. With all the death they had seen, what did it really matter if one more soldier died—particularly a Yankee? Bettie, however, surprised him. Perhaps she even surprised herself. She would take a wagon, she said, hitch up her aging apology for a horse, and try to cross Union lines to the army's supply depot in Harpers Ferry. They would have medicine there, and maybe she could persuade the soldiers to give her some for one of their own. Osborne must have wondered if the privations of war and destitution had finally cost Bettie her sanity.

The trip to Harpers Ferry was twenty miles each way through a war-ravaged stretch of the Shenandoah filled with desperate stragglers and deserters, as well as Mosby's angry raiders. As a woman, Bettie certainly would not have been mistaken by either side for a combatant, but hunger, disease, and a summer of fighting and violent reprisals had begun to fray everyone's nerves. She might be attacked, she might be raped, or she might be shot by pickets by mistake. And, even if she made it, there was certainly no reason to presume that the Union would give her the supplies she needed, or—if they did—what Southern sympathizers would do if they caught her ferrying the medicine to a Yankee officer.

Still, she went. Would they believe her? To prove that she was requesting provisions for a wounded Union soldier and not trying to harvest them for the beleaguered Confederate army, she brought with her a bloodstained letter of Henry Bedell's. Some weeks she went once, some weeks twice. One time she simply challenged the pickets who stopped her at Harpers Ferry: When sentries asked her if the supplies were for a Rebel, she suggested that they return with her to Berryville to see for themselves. She also brought back an enormous amount of whiskey, far more than the patient required. The alcohol was used for diplomatic as well as medicinal purposes: Bettie was bribing the neighbors who knew of her patient—including, quite likely, the Asburys—to remain silent. And silence was critical. Bedell might have been executed if partisans knew of his presence, and even in the Shenandoah, gallantry went only so far. Bettie, too, might be hanged.

For ten days Bettie nursed Bedell in the house where he lay, assisted by her physician and Ginny Runner. They dressed his wounds, they kept the stump that once was his leg free of maggots, they shared with him what little food they had. Then, with the help of four former slaves, Bettie had him carried under the cover of night to her own home a half-mile away, where he could continue his convalescence in a bed. She gave up her own room for Bedell, and she kept the door locked against his inadvertent discovery. Her bedroom was small: a bed, a dresser, a chair, a trunk. But the room was heaven to a soldier who had lain dying on a rubber blanket on a wooden floor.

Why did Bettie do it? Given Bedell's condition when she found him, it certainly wasn't romantic attraction that led her to help him. Was it sympathy engendered because of her own missing husband? The simple compassion a woman might feel for a dying man? Whatever the reason, there can be no doubt that the two grew close.

Through the month of October and the first half of November, they shared the few rooms in her modest home, as he began to regain his strength. One wonders if, over the course of those six weeks, compassion turned gradually to affection. While there is no evidence that the two were lovers, neither is there proof that they weren't. They were two adults with profoundly uncertain futures, living in a secret world of their own construction. That much is clear. They were separated from their spouses, and what might have been unthinkable at other times in their lives might have been irresistible now. Even if they did not become lovers, the faint echoes of their story suggest they cared deeply for each other—at the very least in a manner like siblings or very good friends.

Eventually, given the steady, dependable man Bedell appears in his letters and diary, he must have felt the desire to help out. If he could not tote water from the spring behind the house or find and chop wood for the fire, perhaps he did those chores that would not demand ten fingers or two healthy legs. Maybe he sharpened tools. Perhaps he washed his own clothes— either the remains of his uniform, or pants and shirts he was wearing that belonged to Bettie's husband, James. Virtually any chore would have demanded that he venture outside, and even though the Van Metre home was a half-mile from the nearest house, anytime he was outdoors in daylight both he and Bettie must have been on guard.

At various times while Bedell recuperated, as many as forty renegades were in the area or approaching the house where he lay—though Bettie always kept them in ignorance. By late October, the situation was grim. It's not hard to imagine Bedell up on a makeshift crutch behind the bedroom door, his Colt revolver in his left hand. Perhaps on the other side of the door he could hear the low, angry voices of a group of Mosby's raiders as they confronted Bettie with the rumors they'd heard of Yankee vermin under her roof. The war was not going well for the Confederacy—Atlanta had fallen in early September, and then in October Sheridan had rallied his troops at Cedar Creek and pummeled Early's army—and tempers in the Shenandoah had grown frighteningly short.

Though James van Metre himself was absent, he was not forgotten: While Bettie was at Harpers Ferry obtaining whiskey and medicine, she had received a letter from James from Fort Delaware, the camp where he was a POW. She probably did not share the contents with Bedell, but it does not strain belief to presume that she told the Union officer of its existence. Perhaps it triggered a particular longing in Bedell for his own home, or reassured Bettie that she had done the right thing when she saved this strange Union officer's life. Most likely, it ruptured the fragile private bubble in which they both were living. Bedell was slowly recovering. He and Bettie were now in extreme danger, with each day of his convalescence increasing the chance of discovery.

By early November, he decided that he was strong enough to leave and return to Union lines. He asked Bettie to bring her niece with her and go with him. And she agreed. There was, after all, little left to keep her in the valley now. They had been sliding deeper and deeper into poverty, and she had to know that eventually her neighbors would learn that she had nursed a Union officer back to health. The whiskey she had shuttled from Harpers Ferry could buy her only so much time. And, perhaps, she simply wanted to be with him. Secrecy was key. The consequences would be tragic if Bettie were caught smuggling a Union soldier across Confederate lines.

So Dick Runner took a six-foot-long crockery crate, modified it with air holes and a gun slat, and placed it on the back of a farm wagon that had survived the war. He filled it with straw. And then Bedell climbed inside, taking with him a rifle. Marauders twice stopped the wagon, but Bettie managed to bluff her way through, smiling cheerfully to convince the men she had nothing of value.

Inside his box, Bedell held his rifle at the ready. By afternoon they were safely at the Union camp at Harpers Ferry, where Bedell rose from the crate and was greeted like Lazarus by his fellow troopers, and Bettie was given her rightful due as a hero. But now their roles were reversed and she was the stranger in enemy territory. Their story would take yet another turn. The wounded Bedell could have gone home. But affection and a 19th-century sense of duty and chivalry would not permit it. She had restored him to his loved ones, and he owed nothing less to her now.

Edwin Stanton, Abraham Lincoln's notoriously curmudgeonly Secretary of War, did not spend a lot of time with lowly Union lieutenants. Nor did he entertain the wives of Confederate prisoners with any frequency. But Bedell changed that. In mid-November, he and Bettie met in Stanton's office, always crowded with officers, petitioners and contractors who flooded through wartime Washington. Bedell's description of what occurred in his pension affidavit is a classic in old-fashioned New England understatement: "When I had sufficiently recovered I went to Washington, saw Secretary Stanton, and procured the release of Mr. Van Metre." Walker, in his history, has tears rolling down the Secretary's face as he listened to Bedell describing Bettie's heroism on his behalf. They left Stanton with the assurance they would soon have a letter stating that Fort Delaware's "commanding officer will release any person the bearer may claim as her husband."

James Van Metre originally had been interned at Camp Chase in Ohio in January 1864. But either he had escaped, been recaptured at Spotsylvania four months later and then deposited at Fort Delaware—a makeshift island prison camp the Union created near Delaware City that was known for its appallingly squalid conditions—or he'd simply been transferred from one camp to another in the spring of that year. Either way, in November 1864 there was no record at Fort Delaware of a prisoner named James Van Metre. Consequently, the commander emptied the crudely built barracks for the couple. Prisoner after prisoner filed by.

There were some seventy-seven hundred crammed into Fort Delaware by the final year of the war. Some thirty-two hundred Confederates died there. Envision the scene: A small woman wrapped in a cloak against the chill mid-Atlantic air of November, standing beside a Union officer who—though he was missing a leg—still towers over her. Hundreds of sick, starving, ill-clothed men, who had no idea why, were parading before them. Then as the line of war-ravaged men neared its end, a tall, bearded man with sunken eyes in an emaciated face broke the line and stumbled, weeping, into Bettie's arms. Bettie held him, in tears herself.

Did Bettie experience only elation when she saw James, or was there a flicker of guilt? Did she wonder what her husband would think of her standing beside the man she had nursed and cared for? Although there's no record of James's condition, it's safe to assume that he needed serious nursing. Bedell brought both James and Bettie home with him to Vermont, and they stayed with him until after the war. We'll never know precisely what Bedell and Van Metre shared in their two month's together in the small private universe of the gristmill, or why they did so much for each other. One senses that the spotlight that greeted them in Harpers Ferry was a shock.

What is clear, however, is that each had spouses who loved them deeply. And the bonds between the families grew. When Henry and Emeline had more children, they named two of them, a daughter and a son, after Bettie and James. Soon after the war, the Van Metres took the Bedells to their Virginia home as guests. And forty-five years later, the two couples still remained friends.

In 1915, the Vermont State legislature passed a resolution thanking Bettie for her act of mercy. After their return to Virginia, James was always very protective of his wife—and he needed to be. According to Frank Brumback, a retired physician who is distantly related to Bettie Van Metre, she paid a high price after the war for saving Bedell. "All my Southern relatives considered her a hussy and a traitor," he says. Harry Jones, a retired dairy farmer who grew up in the 1920s in the house James and Bettie built after the war and whose father knew the Van Metres, said the woman was "shunned. She had very limited friends, she was not invited places. She was not well thought of because she'd harbored a Yankee officer." He believes that James was particularly "undone by the way people in the community treated his wife. My father said James would sit on his porch with a gun." Jones does not believe, however, that Bettie went to her grave with any regrets about her decision to save Bedell's life: "She wouldn't have been a complainer or a whiner. Anybody who did what she did must have had real strength."

Henry Bedell and Bettie Van Metre are both buried beside their spouses. Bettie's tombstone is a rectangular slab of gray marble, roughly four feet high and three feet wide. It sits in a cluster of similar headstones on a small hill in the Berryville cemetery. The plot is neat and well tended, with a fourteen-inch-high Maltese cross commemorating James Van Metre's service to the Confederacy. And on occasion one will see, planted beside it in the rich Virginia soil, a pair of flags—one for Vermont, and one whose stars and stripes shine in the Southern sunlight.

CREDITS AND ACKNOWLEDGMENTS

"What They Did for Love," by Andy Simmons, *Reader's Digest*, February 2008.

"All the Days of Your Life," by Neil Simon. Reprinted with permission of Simon & Schuster Publishing Group from *Rewrites: A Memoir*, copyright © 1996; *Reader's Digest*, September 1996.

"To Mend Her Husband's Heart," by John Pekkanen, *Reader's Digest*, March 2001.

"Amazing Love Stories," by Dave Isay. From *All There Is*, copyright © 2012 by Storycorps/Penguin; *Reader's Digest*, February 2012.

"In Sickness, In Health," by Shari Lacy, *Reader's Digest*, June 2004.

"This Thing Called Love," by Maureen Mackey & Bridget Nelson Monroe, *Reader's Digest*, February 2009.

"To Serve With Love," by A. J. Jacobs. From *The Guinea Pig Diaries*, copyright © 2009 by Simon & Schuster; *Reader's Digest*, September 2009.

"A Curious Love Story," by Joseph P. Blank, *Reader's Digest*, March 1975.

"Red Dad, Blue Son," by Joe Hagan, *Reader's Digest*, June 2012.

"The Power of Tattoos," by Lynn Schnurnberger. Copyright © 2011 by Lynn Schnurnberger. *More* magazine, November 2011; *Reader's Digest*, March 2012.

"Married Again . . . With Children," by Wendy Swallow. Copyright © 2002 by Wendy Swallow. *Washingtonian* magazine, February 2002; *Reader's Digest*, November 2002.

"A Life Fully Lived," by Lynn Waldsmith, *Reader's Digest*, February 2000.

"A Very Lucky Daughter," by Sharon Liao. Copyright © 2001 by Sharon Liao. *Washingtonian* magazine, January 2001; *Reader's Digest*, June 2001.

"Friends Interrupted," by Jacquelyn Mitchard, *Reader's Digest*, October 2007.

"Off a Cliff!" by Jeff Rennicke, *Reader's Digest*, February 2010.

"A Winning Friendship," by Molly O'Neill, *Reader's Digest*, October 2005.

"Friends for Life," by Ellen Sherman, *Reader's Digest*, March 2005.

"Bill and Mark: A Tale of Two Friends," by Anne Fadiman. Copyright © 1980 by Time Inc. Reprinted with permission. All rights reserved. *LIFE* magazine (January 1980); *Reader's Digest*, May 1980.

"Puppy Love," by Mary Rowland, *Reader's Digest*, January 2007.

"Mrs. Donovan's Dog," From *All Things Bright and Beautiful* © 1974 by James Herriot. Reprinted by permission of St. Martin's Press. All Rights Reserved. *Reader's Digest*, January 1975.

"A Cop's Best Friend," by Mark Roman, *Reader's Digest*, May 1992.

"Semper Fido," by Lt. Col. Jay Kopelman with Melinda Roth. From *From Baghdad, With Love*, copyright © 2006 by Globe Pequot Press; *Reader's Digest*, December 2013.

"Our Cow Named Tiger Lily," by Penny Porter, *Reader's Digest*, September 1993.

"The Angel for Lost Children," by Barbara Sande Dimmitt, *Reader's Digest*, January 2000.

"This Boy's Life," by Neal Hirschfeld, *Reader's Digest*, September 2001.

"Crossing the Line: A Civil War Love Story," by Chris Bohjalian, *Reader's Digest*, October 2003.

ALSO AVAILABLE FROM READER'S DIGEST

The Best Life Stories

When *Reader's Digest* invited readers to "share a lesson, simple advice, a funny moment, or other story from your life," more than 6,500 people submitted entries. Of those, 150 were carefully selected for this collection. These stories reveal the uncommon wit and wisdom of ordinary people who look at life in extraordinary ways. From poetic to prosaic, heartwrenching to humorous, *The Best Life Stories* proves that every one of us learns lessons worth sharing in our day-to-day struggles, joys, and triumphs.

ISBN 978-1-60652-564-7 • $12.99 hardcover

Stories in Uniform

Tales of courage, hardship, triumph, and enligtenment are echoed over and over in military life, and *Reader's Digest,* the world's best-read magazine, has been chronicling these dramas for over ninety years. In this moving collection of our very best pieces—from World War I through the War on Terror—you'll meet ordinary people faced with extraordinary circumstances in the name of America and freedom. Charged with emotion and packed with unbelievable strength and bravery, *Stories in Uniform* will both engage and inspire you.

ISBN 978-1-62145-063-4 • $15.99 hardcover